BY MARGUERITE YOURCENAR

That Mighty Sculptor, Time

THAT
MIGHTY
SCULPTOR,
TIME

Marguerite Yourcenar

TRANSLATED BY *Walter Kaiser*

IN COLLABORATION WITH THE AUTHOR

The Noonday Press

Farrar, Straus and Giroux

NEW YORK

Library of Congress Cataloging in Publication Data

Yourcenar, Marguerite.

[Temps, ce grand sculpteur. English]

That mighty sculptor, time / Marguerite Yourcenar; translated by

Walter Kaiser in collaboration with the author. — 1st ed.

Translation of: Le temps, ce grand sculpteur.

I. Title.

PQ2649.O8T413 1992   844'.912—dc20   91-27285 CIP

"Tone and Language in the Historical Novel" and "That Mighty Sculptor, Time" first appeared in The New Criterion. "Fires of the Solstice" first appeared in Parabola.

Contents

1

ON SOME
LINES FROM THE
VENERABLE
BEDE

Cume an spearwa . . .

A new cycle begins: like spears, the first green shoots pierce the last dry leaves of the previous autumn. We find ourselves in that time of melting snow and bitter wind when a still almost new Christianity, imported from the East through the mediation of Italy, struggles against an immemorial paganism in the regions of the North, spreading like fire through some ancient forest littered with deadwood; it is the stormy dawn of the seventh century. The most astonishing words which have come down to us on the subject of this change from one faith to another, from the gods to a God, are transmitted through the intermediacy of the Venerable Bede, who recorded them more than a hundred years later, no doubt in his monastery at Jarrow, where, surrounded by a world in turmoil, he composed in Latin his great history of the Christian foundations of England. They were spoken by a thane of Northumberland, who belonged to the powerful Saxon race mixed with Celtic blood which at that time occupied the northern part of the British Isles.

The scene takes place on the outskirts of York, where the buildings of ancient Eburacum, the Roman capital where Septimus Severus died, were still in only the first stage of their existence as ruins; yet they doubtless seemed to the thane and his contemporaries as if out of some timeless antiquity. About two hundred years before, the Emperor Arcadius, in a proclamation to the inhabitants of Britain, had announced that the legions were to recross the sea, leaving them to defend themselves against invaders. Since then, they had made shift as best they could.

Bede put the thane's words into Latin; almost a century and a half had to pass before Alfred the Great, in the free time left him from his struggles against Danish invaders, retranslated this text into an English which was still very close to old Icelandic and various Germanic dialects but which, in the meantime, thanks to the adoption of the Latin alphabet, had acquired the dignity of a written language with a great future before it. If I take the trouble to mention these linguistic vagaries, it is because too few people are aware of the extent to which human speech is relayed to us from the past in stages—staggering along, infected with miscomprehensions, eaten away by omissions, and en-crusted with additions—thanks only to someone like Bede the man of contemplation or Alfred the man of action, who endeavored, despite the almost hopelessly chaotic state of the world, to conserve and transmit what seemed to them worth conserving and transmitting. The brief speech of the thane is, as we shall see, surely one such example.

Edwin, King of Northumberland, at that time the most powerful prince of the British heptarchy, had recently re-ceived a request from a Christian missionary to evangelize in his lands. He summoned his council. As was fitting, the high priest of the local deities, a certain Coifi, was invited to speak first. The language of this divine was more cynical than theological:

"To be frank, Your Highness," he said in effect, "since I have served our gods and presided over our sacrifices, I have been neither happier nor more fortunate than a man who is not devout, and my prayers have rarely been granted.

Therefore, I am in favor of welcoming another god who may be better and stronger, if he can be found."

The priest spoke pragmatically; the leader of the clan who followed spoke as a poet and a seer. Asked to give his opinion on the introduction of a god named Jesus into Northumberland, this thane, whose name is unknown to us, broadened, as it were, the discussion:

"The life of man on earth, My Lord, in comparison with the vast stretches of time about which we know nothing, seems to me to resemble the flight of a sparrow, who enters through a window in the great hall warmed by a blazing fire laid in the center of it where you feast with your councilors and liege men, while outside the tempests and snows of winter rage. And the bird swiftly sweeps through the great hall and flies out the other side, and after this brief respite, having come out of the winter, he goes back into it and is lost to your eyes. Such is the brief life of man, of which we know neither what goes before nor what comes after . . ."

The thane's conclusion accords with that of the priest: since we know nothing, why should we not appeal to those who may know? That point of view is characteristic of an open mind; it leads to the acceptance of certain sublime truths or hypotheses—and sometimes to being taken in by trickery or overthrown by error.

We don't know the opinions of the other members of the council, but these two voices carried the day. The monk Augustine was authorized to preach Christianity in Edwin's lands. The decision (which would have been taken in any case, even had the king's councilors been opposed to it, since it was very much in the air at the time) was pregnant with consequences that still affect us: it carries within it the island monastery of Lindisfarne, that haven of peace and learning in troubled times until the day when the Vikings sunk their axes into the skulls of the monks; it carries within it York Cathedral and Durham, Ely and Gloucester, Saint

Thomas of Canterbury assassinated by the knights of Henry II, and the rich abbeys despoiled by Henry VIII; the Catholicism of Mary Tudor and the Protestantism of Elizabeth, the martyrs on both sides, the thousands of volumes of sermons and devotions, some admirable mystical writings, *The Cloud of Unknowing* and *The Revelations of Divine Love* of Juliana of Norwich, the homilies of John Donne, the meditations of John Law and Thomas Traherne, and, even as I write these lines, the Catholics and Protestants who are shooting each other in the streets of Belfast. The England of Edwin emerges from its Bronze Age to enter the European community, which at that time was indistinguishable from Christianity. After the arrival and departure of the Roman legions and the invasion of the monks from Rome—with all the gains and losses in both cases—a new order once more replaces the old, until that moment when this new order will itself be replaced. No doubt, many of us have wondered how such a changing of the gods was achieved, what doubts and anguished torments preceded it or were born of it, what outbursts of the spirit it occasioned. In the episode described by the Venerable Bede, at least, we observe the grossest cynicism operating undisguisedly on one of the participants, spiced perhaps with a certain love of novelty for its own sake (such a frame of mind is not exclusive to today), and most assuredly with a lively taste for the material goods the new god might bring with him. In the other speaker, whose poetic style is more pleasing to us, there is a deep skepticism which seems to show some profound thought, yet he unhesitatingly trusts the opinions of some newcomer who claims to possess true knowledge. To be sure, one cannot generalize from this one example: this is, in any case, what one pious chronicler tells us about the conversion of King Edwin and his liege men. That absence of reflection which almost always presides over human affairs appears not to have been lacking on this occasion as well.

If the far-reaching effects of this decision were great, its immediate results were uncertain. The high priest Coifi, example par excellence of the zealous turncoat, rushed to the temple in which he officiated and destroyed its idols, thus depriving the museums of the future of some of those barely articulated statues where the stone itself rises, as it were, to the surface and obliterates the awkward human form—as if whatever god depicted there belonged more to the sacred world of minerals than to that of men. Less than three years later, Edwin the Convert was killed on the field of battle by a pagan prince; possibly his ex-high priest and his melancholy thane were killed with him. I don't mean to suggest that, had they been faithful to their former gods, they would have been saved. I would rather believe that the powers on high meant thereby to signify that whoever embraces a faith out of hope for material gain, rather than the spiritual gain it may bring, is deceived. At our great distance from them, we cannot know whether or not those spiritual goods were bestowed on Edwin and his liege men.

. . .

But let us leave there the historical background and the effects of that memorable occasion. Let us look once more at those few phrases of the thane and see what they may still tell us. The metaphor drawn from everyday experience seems to contain within it all the violence and rude comfort of northern winters. Also, and above all, the thane's confession of ignorance remains ours—or rather, would remain so if the philosophies, the techniques, and all the structures man creates and of which he is the prisoner did not hide from the great majority of people today the fact that they know no more about life and death than this leader of a more or less barbaric clan . . . *Adveniensque unus passerum domum citissime pervolaverit, qui cum per unum ostium ingrediens, mox per aliud exierit.* Bede's Latin prose, awkward though it is, is yet still too classical for this primitive thought which is both concrete and vague, more at home in the rough version of Alfred: *Cume an spearwa and hraedlice thaet hus thurhfleo, cume thurh othre duru in, thurh othre ut gewite.* But, for all that, we must take care not to fall into the cliché which would set this mental world, which looks forward across a thousand years to the somber poetic universe of Shakespeare's *Macbeth*, in opposition to the Greco–Latin spirit, which is assumed to be more logical and less lost in the fog of mystery. It is a matter of epoch: a hero out of Homer or an Etruscan lucumo might have spoken the same way.

Looking more closely at this text, which attracts us initially by its beauty alone, we perceive that the thane's thought boldly opposes certain age-old habits of mind which persist even today. Those who, like Vigny, see life as a luminous interval between two infinite periods of darkness readily depict those two shadowy zones of before and after as inert and undifferentiated, a kind of frontier of nothingness. For Christians, despite their belief in a blessed or infernal immortality, what will follow after death (they pay little attention to what came before life) is perceived, above all, as eternal rest. *Invideo, quia quiescunt,* said Luther as he contemplated tombs. For this barbarian, in contrast, the bird issues from a storm and returns into a tempest; these lashings of rain and this wind-tossed snow in the Druidic night make one think of the whirling of atoms or of the whirlwinds of forms in the Hindu sutras. Between these two horrendous storms, the thane interprets the flight of the bird across the hall as a moment of respite (*spatio serenitatis*). That is quite surprising. Edwin's thane knew perfectly well that a bird which has flown into a house of men darts about madly, running the risk of dashing itself against those incomprehensible walls, of burning itself in the fire, or of being snapped up by the hounds lying next to the hearth. Life as we know it is hardly a moment of respite.

Yet the image of the bird come out of nowhere and gone

back into nowhere is a fine symbol for man's brief and inexplicable passage on earth. One might even go further and make another, equally poignant symbol of the hall besieged by snow and wind, lit up for a brief moment in the depths of the mournful grayness of winter: a symbol for the brain, that lighted chamber, that generating fire, placed for each of us temporarily at the center of things, without which neither the bird nor the storm would be either imagined or perceived.

1976

2

SISTINE

Gherardo Perini

The Maestro said to me:
"Here is the boundary stone at the crossroads, some two miles from the Porta del Popolo. We are already so distant from the City that those who depart laden with memories have almost forgot Rome by the time they arrive here. For men's memory resembles those weary travelers who disencumber themselves of some useless baggage at each stop. So that they arrive naked, with their hands empty, at the place where they are to sleep, and on the day of the great awakening will be like infants who know nothing of yesterday. Gherardo, here is the boundary stone. The dust of the roads has blanched the few trees which stand in the Campagna like God's milestones; near here, there is a cypress tree whose roots are exposed, which has difficulty surviving. There is also an inn, where people go to drink. I imagine that wealthy, protected women come here on weekdays to give themselves to their lovers, and that on Sundays families of poor workingmen celebrate by taking a meal here. I imagine that, Gherardo, because it is the same everywhere.

"I shall not go any further, Gherardo. I shall not accompany you further, because my work is pressing and I am old. I am an old man, Gherardo. Sometimes, when you wish to be more tender than usual, you call me your father. But I have no children. I have never met a woman as beautiful as my figures in stone, a woman who could stay motionless for hours, without speaking, like some essential thing which has no need to act in order to be and which causes you to forget the passage of time because she is always there. A woman who allows herself to be looked at without smiling, without blushing, because she knows that beauty is a grave matter. The women in stone are chaster than the others, and above all more faithful; only they are sterile. There is no fissure where pleasure, death, or the seed of a child can enter into them, and that is why they are less fragile. Yet sometimes they break, and their entire beauty remains contained in each fragment, like God in all things; but nothing alien enters into them to make their hearts explode with joy. Imperfect beings become agitated and couple in order to complete themselves, but purely beautiful things are as solitary as the grief of man. Gherardo, I have no children. And I am well aware that most men do not really have sons: they have a Tito, or a Caio, or a Pietro, but that is not the same joy. If I had a son, he would not resemble the image I had formed of him before he came into existence. In the same way, the statues I make are different from those I had dreamt of at first. But God keeps for Himself the right to be the knowing creator.

"If you were my son, Gherardo, I would not love you more; I just would not have to ask myself why I loved you. All my life I have looked for answers to questions that perhaps have no answers; I have burrowed into marble as if truth could be found in the heart of stones, and I have spread colors over walls as if I were plastering chords of music onto too vast a silence. For everything keeps silence, even our soul—or else it is that we cannot hear.

"And so, you are departing. I am no longer young enough to attach importance to a separation, even if it is definitive.

I know too well that the beings we love and who love us best are imperceptibly departing from us at every moment that passes. It is in this way that they part from themselves. You are sitting on this boundary stone, and you believe you are still here; but your being, already turned towards the future, no longer belongs to your life that was, and your absence has already begun. Oh, I know that all that is only an illusion like the rest, and that there is no future. Man, who invented time, then invented eternity for contrast; but the negation of time is as vain as time itself. There is no past or future, only a series of successive presents, a road perpetually destroyed and continued, upon which we all go forward. You are sitting down, Gherardo, but your feet are placed on the ground in front of you with a kind of restlessness, as if they were testing out some route. You are clothed in the garments of our era, which will seem hideous, or simply strange, when our era is past, because clothing is never anything more than a caricature of the body. I see you naked. I have the gift of seeing the radiance of the body through clothing, in the same way, I suppose, that saints see into souls. It is a torture when they are ugly; when they are beautiful, it is another sort of torture. You are beautiful, with that fragile beauty that life and time lay siege to on every side and will finally take from you; but for this moment it is yours, and yours it will remain on the vault of the church where I have painted your image. Even if one day your mirror gives you back nothing more than a deformed portrait in which you do not have the courage to recognize yourself, there will always be, somewhere, an unchanging reflection which will resemble you. In the same way, I shall fix your soul.

"You no longer love me. If you consent to listen to me for this hour, it is because one is indulgent towards those one is abandoning. You bound me to you, and now you are unbinding me. I do not blame you, Gherardo. A person's love is such an unexpected gift, and so little deserved, that we should always be surprised that it is not taken back sooner. I am not troubled by those you do not yet know but towards whom you are going and who perhaps await you: the person they will know will be different from the one I believed I knew and think I love. No one possesses anyone (even sinners cannot achieve that), and since art is the only true possession, it is less a matter of possessing than of re-creating a person. Do not misunderstand my tears, Gherardo: it is better that those we love should go while we are still able to weep for them. If you were to stay, perhaps your presence, superimposing itself, would weaken the image of that presence I want to preserve. Just as your clothing is but the envelope of your body, you are no longer anything for me but the envelope of that other person whom I have disengaged from you and who will live long after you. Gherardo, you are now more beautiful than yourself.

"One possesses for all eternity only the friends from whom one has parted."

Tommai dei Cavalieri

I am Tommai dei Cavalieri, a young lord, passionate about art. Handsome as I am, my soul is nevertheless even more beautiful, in such manner that my body, painted on the vault of a church, is nothing more than the geometric sign of rectitude and fidelity. I am sitting, my hand on my knee, in the pose of someone who rises with ease. The Maestro, who loves me, has painted, sketched, or sculpted me in all the postures life imprints on us, but I had sculpted myself before he did. What shall I do? To what god, hero, or woman shall I dedicate this masterpiece, myself?

What shall I do? Perfection is a road that leads only to solitude: I no longer see in men anything but surmounted rungs. The Maestro, who has greater genius than I, is in my presence nothing more than a poor man no longer in possession of himself, and Michelangelo would gladly exchange his ardor for my serenity. What shall I do? Have I sharpened my soul only to have a sword I shall not brandish? . . . That mad emperor wished that the world had only one head, so that he could cut it off. Would that it were only one body, that I might embrace it; one fruit, that I might pluck it; one enigma, which I might finally solve. Shall I seize an empire? Shall I construct a temple? Shall I write a poem, which will last longer? The parceling out of action disillusions me from acting, and each victory is nothing more than a broken mirror in which I cannot see myself whole. One has to have too many illusions to desire power, too much vanity to desire glory. Since I possess myself, what enrichment could the universe bring me—and happiness means nothing to me.

When men contemplate my picture, they will not ask who I was or what I did: they will praise me for having existed. I am seated on the capital of a column, as if at the top of the world, and am myself its crown. O life, vertiginous imminence! He for whom everything is possible does not need to attempt anything.

Cecchino dei Bracchi

I, Michelangelo, dresser of stone, I have painted on this vault the image of a youth of Florence who was dear to me and is no more. He is sitting in a fierce attitude, and his crossed arms seem to hide his heart. But perhaps the dead have a secret they do not want you to know.

At first, I loved my dreams, because I knew nothing else. Then I loved my family (which was, as I think back on it, as if I loved myself) and the friends I acquired, who were laden with so much beauty that I was both humiliated and made happy by it. And, finally, I loved a woman. My parents are dead; my friends, my loved ones have departed: some have left me to live, others possibly for the betrayal of the tomb. I am not sure of those who remain; even if my suspicions are not justified, I suffer as much as if they were, because everything always takes place in the mind. The woman I loved, she, too, has departed from this world, like a stranger who discovers that she has come to the wrong door and that her own house is elsewhere. Hence, I went back to loving only my dreams, because nothing else was left to me. But dreams, too, can betray, and now I am alone.

We love because we are not able to endure being alone.

For the same reason, we fear death. Whenever I have proclaimed aloud the love another being inspired in me, I have seen all around me the winking eyes and the shaking heads, as if those who heard me thought themselves my accomplices or permitted themselves to be my judges. Those who do not accuse you seek to excuse you, and that is even sadder. For example, I loved a woman. When I say that I have loved only one woman, I am not speaking about those others, those passersby, who are not women but only female flesh. I have loved only one woman, for whom I had no desire—and when I think back, I can't remember whether that was because she was not beautiful enough or because she was too beautiful. But people don't understand how beauty can be an obstacle, sating desire in advance. Even those we love do not understand that, or do not wish to. They are amazed; they suffer; they resign themselves. Then they die. Thus, we begin to fear that our renunciation has been a sin against ourselves, and our desire, lacking an outlet, having become as unreal and obsessive as a ghost, takes on the monstrous aspect of everything that has never existed. Of all man's regrets, perhaps the cruelest is that for the unachieved.

To love someone is not only to want that person to live; it is also to be astonished when he ceases to live, as if death were something unnatural. And yet, being is a more astonishing miracle than non-being; if you think about it, it is before the living that one must bow and kneel, as before an altar. I suppose nature gets tired of resisting nothingness, just as man tires of resisting the enticements of chaos. In my existence, which, as I grow older, is plunged into more and more crepuscular periods, I have continually seen the forms of perfect life strive to give way to others more simple, closer to primitive humility, in the way that mud is older than granite; and whoever carves statues only hastens, after all, the crumbling of mountains. The bronze of my father's tomb becomes coated with verdigris in the courtyard of a village church; the picture of that youth of Florence will begin to flake off the vault I have painted; the poems I wrote for the woman I loved will, in a few years, no longer be understood—and for poems, that is a form of death. The wish to immobilize life is the sculptor's damnation. It is in that respect, perhaps, that all my work is contrary to nature. At every instant, the marble in which we think we have preserved a form of perishable life returns to its place in nature, through erosion, patina, and the play of light and shadow over planes which thought they were abstract but are in fact only the surface of a stone. In the same way, no doubt the eternal mutability of the universe astonishes its Creator.

Before she was put into her coffin, I kissed the hand of the only woman who, for me, gave meaning to the whole of life; but I did not kiss her lips, and now I regret that, since her lips might have taught me something. Nor did I kiss the youth of Florence, neither his hands nor his pale face. Only, I do not regret that. He was too beautiful. He was perfect, like those whom nothing can touch; for the dead are all impassive. I have seen many dead. My father, having rejoined his ancestors, was no more than an anonymous Buonarroti; he had laid down the burden of being himself; he had effaced himself, in the humility of death, to the point of being no more than a name in a long series of men; his line no longer ended with him, but with me, his successor, for the dead are only the terms of a problem posed by each of their living continuers, one after another. The woman I loved, after the fatal illness which shook her as though it would uproot her soul, retained a hard, triumphant smile on her lips, as if, victorious over life, she silently despised her vanquished adversary; and I witnessed her pride in having crossed over into death. Cecchino dei Bracchi, my friend, was simply handsome. His beauty, which so many gestures and thoughts had, while he lived, fragmented into expressions or movements, became once more intact, absolute, eternal: one would have said that he had composed his body before leaving it. I saw smiles lift the corners of his bloodless lips, glimmer beneath his closed eyelids, and flood his face with the equivalent of light. The dead lie quiet, satisfied, knowing that nothing can destroy, since death cancels itself out even as it achieves its purpose. And because they have gone beyond knowledge, I have assumed that they understood.

But perhaps the dead do not understand that they understand.

Febo del Poggio

I am awakening. What did the others say? Dawn, you who reconstruct the world each morning; complete, with naked arms that hold the universe; youth, the dawn of man. What does it matter to me what others have said, thought, believed . . . I am Febo del Poggio, a scoundrel. Those who speak of me say that I have a base soul; but perhaps I have no soul at all. I exist in the way a piece of fruit exists, a glass of wine, a splendid tree. When winter comes, one abandons the tree that no longer offers shade; when one's hunger is sated, one throws away the pit; when the glass is empty, one takes another. I accept that. Summer, the lustral water of morning over lithe limbs; O joy, dew of the heart . . .

I am awakening. Before me, behind me, there is eternal night. For millions of ages I have slept; for millions of ages I shall sleep again . . . I have but one hour. Why would you spoil it with explanations or maxims? I stretch out in the sun, on the pillow of pleasure, in a morning that will never again return.

1931

3

TONE AND LANGUAGE IN THE HISTORICAL NOVEL

It has not been sufficiently emphasized that although we possess an enormous mass of written documents, and also visual documents, from the past, nothing is left to us of *voices* before the first nasal-sounding phonograph records of the nineteenth century. What is more, as far as the representation of speech is concerned, nothing, or virtually nothing, was achieved before certain great novelists or dramatists of the nineteenth century. By that, I mean that they were the first to register *conversation* in all its spontaneity, its disjointed logic, its complex byways, its lacunae, and its unarticulated implications without passing through tragic or comic stylization or lyric outburst.

Neither antiquity nor any of the intervening centuries offers us the equivalent of a conversation between Pierre Bezukhov and Prince Andrei in Tolstoy, between Ibsen's Rosmer and Rebecca West and her wily brother-in-law, or—at opposite ends of the spectrum—Vautrin's words as he propounds his views on life to Lucien, or the brief interchange between Marcel and the doctor who comes to listen to his grandmother's heartbeat. The transcription of speech in terms of pure realism, without any sort of bias, is curiously contemporaneous with those two mechanical means of reproducing the object as it is, the phonograph and the photograph.

Mutatis mutandis, the same observations can be made about the unspoken words which take shape within us under the sudden impact of an experience—Rastignac's impressions as he looks out over Paris from the heights of Père-Lachaise, the last thoughts that cross Anna Karenina's mind, the feelings of Prince Andrei as he lies wounded on the battlefield at Austerlitz. It follows that, for every novelistic attempt at re-creation, the representation of these various *unstylized* forms of speech constitutes an enormous stumbling block. One may indeed wonder if the methods used to achieve this in the novel as it developed in Europe in the nineteenth and the beginning of the twentieth century aren't really meaningless when applied to an earlier period. One may especially wonder if the fact that the ancients themselves have left nothing of this sort doesn't prove that the form of the novel is badly adapted to evoking ancient sensibility.

Let us look again at those literary texts out of which emerge, so to speak, the sounds and spoken rhythms of that period which extends roughly from Pericles to Julian the Apostate, a period of about eight centuries. The philosophical dialogue was a Greek genre par excellence, subsequently a Latin one by imitation: in it, literary conventions are, naturally, combined with dialectic conventions. It is only here and there, in brief passages (mostly in prologues or epilogues) meant to give the reader a rest, that Plato, with an admirable artistry (and I underscore the word *artistry*), slips in some short exchanges which might be those of contemporary conversation. The great tragedians, by definition, use a tragic style, itself often derived from the archaic terms and turns of phrase of epic language. The dialogues of comedy are often confined either to the language of humble people (one could write an entire essay on the amused condescension of comic authors in every era who reproduce, each in his own way, popular speech) or, more rarely, to the parody of polished language, such as the public believes is spoken. The utterances of Socrates in *The Clouds* are like the arguments of Bergson or Gabriel Marcel translated into popular jokes. Menander and Terence give their characters a language of bourgeois correctness, somewhat colorless, which was later imitated everywhere by the "high comedy" of the seventeenth and eighteenth centuries—a language which has never been spoken outside of the theater. The mimes offer us observations of an exquisite realistic precision, but, once again, based on ironic condescension: Herondas and Theocritus look down on their panders and gossips from a great height. The picaresque novel, of which we have only two examples, Petronius and Apuleius, sometimes has the limitations of mime, sometimes those of a "good joke" or popular tale.

Certain elegiac or lyric poems tell us something about the tone of voice in which emotions were spoken, cried out, or sung. We feel that that cry of passion in Theocritus's *Sorceress* must have been uttered more or less in that way. Without doubt, even overly literary works like Ovid's *Art of Love* supply us with something of the tone of flirtatious conversations—all the more so as that sort of conversation is based on conventions. Here and there the Greek epigrammatists open clear vistas: six verses of Callimachus sum up what an intellectual faced with suicide must have thought and therefore said; the foreign slave asking to be buried according to his native rites, in an epigram of Dioscorides, must have spoken almost like that. Yet, once again, we find that *decantation* which is the characteristic, in itself admirable, of ancient literature: the poet serves as a sort of filter. Satirists exaggerate by profession. Some of Martial's epigrams give us the tone of Roman gossip; the broadside of insults directed against Caesar by Catullus must have been mouthed by many of Pompey's partisans; yet these versified obscenities are still literature.

The historians also simplify and schematize, distancing themselves, if not from the deeds (and who has better described deeds than Thucydides?), at least from the hubbub of words surrounding those deeds. We know that they undertook to rewrite the debates they inserted into their work, in order to make them express what the orator might have or ought to have said. Even less do we hear the tumult of an assembly in their works; yet stenographic transcripts existed; but it would have been contrary to their concept of history to have reproduced them as they were. Their purpose is, in effect, exemplary, as it is with Plutarch or (in another sense and *a contrario*) with Tacitus; or else analytic, as it is with Thucydides and Polybius. It is rarely, if ever, the reality of an incident seized at the moment, and even less the reality of verbal exchange and voice. Suetonius gives us the written equivalent of those realistic Roman portrait busts of private citizens and statesmen; but from that series of traits of character or of manners scarcely a spoken word emerges, and never so much as a fragment of conversation. To be sure, from time to time a "historic utterance," whether authentic or not (and I would maintain that at this distance authenticity is of little importance), causes us to hear a voice almost always raised to the diapason of a cry, or else some decisive words which sum up a situation and are engraved, as it were, for the posterity of all time (*Tu quoque, Brute* . . . , *Qualis artifex pereo* . . . , *Alea jacta est* . . .). We hear them, so to speak, in a void, isolated from whatever words or cries preceded or followed them —the angry interjections of the conspirators as they fall on Julius Caesar, the terrified murmur of the poor women and faithful slaves around Nero, the excited conversations of the officers and men as they crossed the Rubicon with their leader. In the exceedingly mediocre *Life of Commodus* in the *Historia Augusta*, the decree condemning Commodus to the Scalae Gemoniae stuns us, because it makes us feel palpably the enormous surge of hatred that swept over the senators as they looked on the dead emperor. It is one of the rare cases where the rumbling of a mob can be heard across the centuries.

Happily, there are sub-literary documents (that which I've just cited is one of them) which haven't undergone the filtering or rearranging literature entails. Legal judgments or decrees, such as the senatorial warrants or decisions punishing with death participation in the Bacchanalia, which cause us brutally to experience the terror of the people inculpated; letters of private citizens which furnish us with the tone of a student apologizing for having wrecked the family chariot or of a soldier asking his family to send him a care package; the letters of Cicero and Pliny, more consciously belonging to the "epistolary genre," which tell us something about written communications in upper-class society; graffiti which contain the scrawled echo of the talk and shouts of the street. They are voices out of the past, some of them practically in their raw state, each of them giving us the faint shock of the unexpected; yet there is nothing in them that would have enabled me to re-create with even a minimum of plausibility an exchange about serious or urgent, subtle or complex matters, a conversation between Hadrian and Trajan, or Plotina, or Antinous, or with his legate Severus concerning the affairs of Judaea. Nothing, or virtually nothing, is left us of those inflections, those quarter tones, those articulated half smiles which yet can change everything.

I shall inflict only one example upon the reader: I caused Hadrian to report, in scarcely amplified form, an incident which is recounted in a few words in a chronicle: the emperor, ill, had asked a doctor for some poison, and the doctor killed himself in order not to have to refuse the request. At the outset, the novelist adds to this skeletal news item a few details she hopes are plausible: the emperor's sympathy for the young doctor ("I took pleasure in his intelligence, both daring and dreamy, and in the dark fire of those deep-set eyes"); the subterfuges used to persuade the chief doctor, Hermogenes, from whom the emperor could not hope for this ultimate help, to go spend the day in Rome, thus leaving the sick man in the care of his young assistant ("An excuse came for me to get rid of Hermogenes for several hours: he had to examine candidates for the chair of medicine which I had just founded at the Odeon"); the interview which, on Hadrian's part, ends in supplications ("I insisted; I made absolute demand; I employed every means to try to arouse his pity, or to corrupt him; he will be the last man whom I shall have implored"); the equivocal response of the doctor ("Finally won over, he promised me to go and seek the dose of poison. I awaited him in vain until evening. Late in the night I learned with horror that he had just been found dead in his laboratory, with a glass phial in his hands"). I believe the tone of this passage to be more or less correct. But suppose I had tried to present these actions and conversations directly? I know that I would have fallen into error, into melodrama or pastiche, or both. In this regard, popular literature alternates between the servile copying of a few ancient expressions known to everyone ("Full, I am full," says the drunken patrician in the old French operetta . . . "Bear these wingèd words to Metella") and the homespun ingenuity of Technicolor scenarios ("Spartacus, I think I am going to have a baby"). Someone will say that Corneille in *Cinna*, Racine in *Britannicus*, and Shakespeare in *Julius Caesar* managed it all rather well. But that is, of course, because they possessed genius. It is also—and perhaps even more to the point—because they were not concerned with *tonal authenticity*.

Without having compiled the preceding catalogue, I chose to make Hadrian use a dignified form of speech (*oratio togata*). Different though they are from each other, and whether they are called *Commentaries, Meditations, Epistles, Treatises*, or *Discourses*, the greatest works of the Greek and Latin prose writers who come before or immediately after

Hadrian all belong more or less within this category of sustained style, half narrative, half meditative, but always essentially *written*, from which immediate impressions and sensations are virtually excluded and from which any verbal exchange is ipso facto banished. Obviously, it was not a question here of imitating Caesar or Seneca, or even Marcus Aurelius, but of deriving from them a pattern, a rhythm, the equivalent of a piece of fabric which one subsequently drapes as one will over the nude model. The "style of the toga" would provide the emperor with that dignity without which we cannot imagine antiquity—wrongly, no doubt, yet also with some reason, for dignity was one of man's ideals down to the end of antiquity: as he lay dying, Caesar arranged the folds of his toga. This style allowed me to eliminate those minima which are proverbially eschewed by the praetor. The sounds of spoken exchanges fell away by themselves: there was no more question of Hadrian's recounting his conversation with Osroes than of Caesar's having thought to put in writing his discussion with Vercingetorix. Even better, the *oratio togata* allowed me to present Hadrian addressing—beyond his contemporaries and his adopted grandson—an ideal interlocutor, *Man himself*, who has been the enticing chimera for all civilizations down to our time. He thereby addresses us.

But to speak of an address is also to speak of monologue; and it was at that level that I finally found the voice. Possibly that observation has more significance for Hadrian than for us, since in that epoch a man reading alone, and no doubt *writing* alone, read or wrote *aloud*. In attempting to rediscover that voice through the deliberate form of an address, I used the little—but the diverse little—that is left from Hadrian himself. We possess no more than three lines of the *Memoirs* he dictated to or had composed by an amanuensis, which no doubt constituted only a very official résumé of his life. Nevertheless, the man who admits therein to having got drunk as a youth at Trajan's table in order to curry favor with him was surely not a man who shrouded everything in lies; the strategist who, in an address to his troops, described with a refined precision their movements on a day of maneuvers reveals the intellectual beneath the general-in-chief. I tried to synthesize a series of strict legal or administrative decrees emanating from the head of state with the casual, light verses of the great amateur who, although he preferred the most difficult poets, seems himself willingly to have turned to the popular poetry of his day when he wrote his own verse. I had to make the best use I could of three intimate letters which are perhaps authentic and which, even if they aren't, at least show how at that time people thought Hadrian expressed himself. One, gay and playful, to his mother-in-law; another, detached, to a brother-in-law who was also his secret enemy; the third, very dignified, to his successor. A few writings by contemporaries who were part of his circle also seem, at moments, to refract his voice. Arrian (if it is indeed he), addressing Hadrian in his *Periplus of the Black Sea*, gives an example of the tender allusions his familiars made to the emperor on the subject of the dead and deified Antinous. The folklore gathered more or less from everywhere by Phlegon, his secretary, shows us the topics, if not the tone, of the casual conversations at table and at the end of a day's journey. The list of administrative divisions of Antinoopolis, charged with religious and mystical significance, carries us back to the orders given in his own voice by Hadrian for the founding of that city.

But perhaps those rare *spoken words* embedded in the heavy dough of the chronicles helped me even more: the retorts, some of a military brusqueness, others of an Italian finesse; the curt, lofty remark of the husband admitting that he would have got divorced "had he been a private citizen"; the bitter reflections of the aged man who cites Virgil at the deathbed of his heir (*Tu Marcellus eris . . . Purpureos spargam flores*) but refuses the dead man official honors and grieves above all for himself ("All that has already cost the state too much money . . . I leaned against a crumbling wall"); the irritated complaint of the sick man ("The doctors have killed me!") whose last motto was nonetheless *Patientia*. Very little to go on: bits of voice out of which to reconstitute an entire tone or timbre of voice, the way others reconstitute a broken statue out of fragments of marble. And someone may say that tone and timbre here are nothing other than temperament, comportment, or character traits. I would agree. If the language of our characters is so important, that is because it expresses or betrays them completely.

I don't flatter myself that I always succeeded. A passage that delights many readers, the almost lyric description of Hadrian's voyages with Antinous through Greece and Asia, seems to me now a piece of bravura, an aria which focuses on what I have Hadrian call the summit of his years of happiness. I still believe that the emperor, retrospectively calling up his memories, could have seen them that way, vividly colored like the large frescos at Herculaneum, stylized like the bas-reliefs of his hunts on the medallions of the future Arch of Constantine. But I no longer believe that he would have recounted them in quite that fashion—or, if so, am I then to suppose that at that moment he would plunge into a sort of Propertian or Tibullan elegy, making use, as it were, of all the resources of literature? I don't hold the passage against him, or against myself. It is always difficult to recount a moment of happiness.

I had the opportunity to verify, as if with a touchstone, the authenticity of another passage. A professor asked his students to translate into Greek (I should like to be able to say *retranslate*) that page where the emperor describes the state of atony which overcame him after the death of Antinous. I attempted it as well. Immediately, the *addenda* in a more modern tone became as discernible as the plaster which joins two fragments of a statue. Let me cite the passage, putting in italics the part which, quite definitely, does not work: "The journey up the river continued, but my course lay on the Styx. In prisoners' camps on the banks of the Danube I had once seen wretches continually beating their heads against a wall *with a wild motion, both mad and tender*, endlessly repeating the same name. In the underground chambers of the Colosseum I had been shown lions pining away because the dog with which their keepers had accustomed them to live had been taken away. I tried to collect my thoughts: Antinous was dead . . ." Eight words refused to be written in Greek; they could have been written a bit more easily in Latin, a language which already underscores emotions as ours does. But in which language had I imagined that Hadrian, who was bilingual, was dictating his *Memoirs* to me? No doubt, sometimes in Latin and sometimes in Greek—which gave me a certain freedom. Yet there are moments when, inadvertently, I caused him to speak the French of my day, and these eight words seem to me, as I reread them, to constitute one such moment. The reader will ask why I do not then remove them. Because the impression, if not the expression, seems authentic to me, and because I regard inexactitude a bit the way the emperor, in my opinion, regarded risk; that is: after all precautions have been taken, it is right to let inexactitude play its part, and even to welcome the enrichments it may bring us. On condition, of course, that that part should be as small as possible.

Before leaving the emperor, I should like to protest against an adjective I too often see affixed to the title *Memoirs of Hadrian* in articles that are otherwise full of praise—*apocryphal*. *Apocryphal* is used, or should only be used, for what is false and tries to pass as true. The ballads of Ossian composed by Macpherson were apocryphal because they pretended to be by Ossian. Fraud is implicit in the word. My observation is neither irritable nor, it seems to me, trifling: that improper adjective (it would be better to speak of *Imaginary Memoirs*) indicates how little critics, and the public, are accustomed to the passionate reconstitution, at once detailed and free, of a moment or a man out of the past.

.   .   .

The Abyss is polyphonic rather than monodic. It contains many conversations, from brief exchanges of a practical nature—yet inevitably charged with some emotional poten- tial—to meandering dialogues where two interlocutors in agreement, or in partial disagreement, pass an idea back and forth between them in perfect trust, or, on the contrary, through double and triple layers of dissembled thought. Unlike *Memoirs of Hadrian*, the book is not written in the first person: that is to say, its world is not seen and described by one central character. In fact, just as I had felt early on that the tone of *Memoirs of Hadrian* would gain in accuracy from passing through the voice of the emperor, I quickly perceived that in *The Abyss* the contrast between the tone of voice of a modern narrator and that of characters from another century would be intolerable, and that the narrated parts should be done as much as possible in the indirect style, sometimes passing through Zeno himself or some other major or minor character, sometimes through "the voice of the people," as if through a muffled and almost always half-witted choral whispering. Life reconsidered by Hadrian from the perspective of memory gave way to life experienced from day to day at a level very close to the level of spoken language.

Up to a point, the literary style of the sixteenth century helped me with its concreteness and directness and a spec- ificity it had inherited in part from one aspect of the Middle Ages. But verbal exchanges as such are as rare as they are in the literature of antiquity. The Latin dialogues of Eras- mus are to the highest degree *written*. Those of Aretino furnish a mine of information about the low-life of his time, but they belong to the genre, which abounds everywhere, of the more or less satirical rendering of popular life. Italian comedy is highly stylized. The actual "words" reported by the chroniclers of the time mostly consist, as with the ancients, not of bits of conversation but of memorable phrases like that response (so fine because so immediate) made by the wife of the Admiral de Coligny to her husband, who had given her two weeks to make a dangerous decision: "The two weeks are already over, sir." ("My husband, the fortnight is already passed" from the mouth of Hilzonde in *The Abyss* echoes this, in a similar situation.) The same is true of the odious jokes uttered by the German Schopp at Bruno's execution, which I borrowed for Zeno's trial. Only Shakespeare and, here and there, his Elizabethan emulators give us—but a generation after the date when *The Abyss* ends—the lively tone of verbal exchanges in the sixteenth century, at least in those passages where a certain rhetoric hasn't smothered them. But that passionate rhetoric is itself characteristic of the time: some of the lyrical soliloquies of Lear or Hamlet, which audibly belong to the world of the theater, nonetheless tell us something about the language for emotions violently felt by certain especially strong or thoughtful people. They shed a light on the thinking, feeling men at the end of that century which we don't have again in the same intensity for any other era before our own.

There is a constant shifting between the written and the spoken in certain works of the sixteenth century. Not in all, of course: the humanists who copied antiquity destroyed scholastic routines of thought and expression, but only to create others, essentially oratorical, which have sometimes lasted down to our time. Those works we still read, in any case, are very close to the oral mode. When we read Montaigne, we often feel we are silently participating in a unilateral conversation; all the freshness and rudeness of common speech is in Luther. The exchange of indignant letters between Agrippa of Nettesheim and an honest curate of Metz on the subject of a scandalous Inquisition affair has all the heat of oral testimony. In the *Journal* which Dürer kept as a strictly personal memorandum and in more of a spoken than a written style, his notes on the death of his mother burst from the page in the midst of his financial accounts and descriptions of wayside lodgings, and we are haunted by the mixture of sketches and incomplete phrases he jotted down when he awoke from a nightmare.

Beyond such intimate works, we encounter the secret ones. Privately, in his mirror writing, Leonardo composed *Notebooks* which were for him alone; and the fact that they have appeared only by accident some three centuries later gives us the feeling of entering, unencumbered by any intermediary interpretation, into the very interior of a man of genius making a record of himself without any witnesses. They are unliterary notebooks, for Leonardo was even more of an autodidact than Zeno; yet they achieve the poetry of pure *tone*, like everything that comes directly from the self. Some of the secret reports of the ambassadors of Venice have the sound of a whispering voice. The soiled pages, in an Italian jargon besmirched with Latin, of the scribe who put down in writing the incoherent mumblings of Campanella when he was being subjected to torture, or those of the informer who noted down the words the philosopher exchanged with his friend Fra Pietro Ponzio in prison, seem even more literally slices of life, cries torn from a man thrashing about in anguish and the clandestine echo of a conversation that was already clandestine. In their time, they were shown only to the rather distracted or astute eyes of the judges; then they were buried in the judicial archives of the Kingdom of Naples until their publication in 1886. Yet it seems as though their specific horror has not evaporated in the slightest in the time between the actual event and now. In *The Abyss*, I made no use of the first of these documents, having spared Zeno torture in order to avoid any touch of melodrama; from the second I took only the affectionate Fra Pietro's *eamus ad dormiendum* and his *cor meum*, which Zeno hears murmured out of the depths of his past by the voice of another friend a quarter of an hour before his death. Yet no other piece of writing has ever so vividly brought me the *auditory* shock of the crumbling of the walls of time.

The fact that we still have an oral knowledge of the language, or rather the languages, that Zeno speaks (for if Hadrian is bilingual, Zeno is polyglot), which we shall never have of the Latin and Greek of the second century, contributed to this drift toward spoken language in *The Abyss*. Despite the fact that French changed, mostly for the worst and in the direction of a narrowing and constraining propriety, between about 1550 and the present, many of my characters' phrases would still have come into my mouth just as they were. At the risk of creating the impression of excessive meticulousness, I confess to having turned to dictionaries for every doubtful word—that is, for each word which I suspected had entered the language after the sixteenth century or, at most, after the beginning of the seventeenth; and those words I ruthlessly suppressed because they carried with them ideas that my characters could not have had in that form. With almost equal care, I did my best to avoid as much as possible every word which had ceased to be in common usage after the end of the sixteenth century and which I might have been tempted to use out of a love for the picturesque or the archaic, with no other valid psychological reason. It is because of words or phrases inserted to give a sense of period that the "historical novel" disqualifies itself, as often as it does because of anachronisms.

Let me give a few examples. The word *Protestant* is used from time to time from the beginning of the sixteenth century, but it still wavers imperceptibly between its current meaning (a member of a Christian religion) and its meaning as an active participle (a man who protests); and subsequently it is laden for the reader with meanings that come from more recent stages of Protestantism. It is above all in its meaning of an armed faction that it is used in *The Abyss*, as is the word *Catholic* as well ("the Protestant princes," "our Catholics"). *Huguenot* is meaningful only against a French background, and the characters of this novel live mostly in the lands of the Holy Roman Empire; moreover, it is almost as aggressively archaic a word as *rapier*. The words *Lutherans, Calvinists*, and *Anabaptists*, which have a narrower focus, are more useful for our particular subject: they indicate to what degree these groups were still perceived as separate, sometimes violently divergent, not yet fused into an entity perceived from without as monolithic. The same observation applies to *Iconoclasts*, which sometimes designates Anabaptists, sometimes Calvinists, sometimes both, and which gives us nothing more than what the bourgeoisie of large Flemish towns deigned to know about some dangerous rebels. "Members of the supposedly Reformed Religion" is an adequate designation on the lips of ecclesiastics and jurists. When I looked into some of the translations of *The Abyss*, I discovered that Captain Henry Maximilian spoke of syphilis like a twentieth-century sociologist, instead of referring to the good old pox of the soldier; the fact that the learned word figures in a Latin allegory composed by a doctor of the period makes no difference, since it became a word of common usage only much later, and then initially as a euphemism. The word *bugger* suffered a good deal at the hands of some of my translators. Some prudishly rendered it as *heretic*, which wouldn't have been right except in the twelfth or thirteenth century; others made it into a sort of *good old chap*, much too modern, even though the word must have rapidly slipped into that sort of meaning. The sexual significance eluded them, even though it was present in the usage of the sixteenth and seventeenth centuries. *Patriot*, which acquires currency only in the eighteenth century, would have been ridiculous in popular speech around 1550, yet it's often found in the *Chronicles of the Troubles in the Low Countries*. Anticipating by at least two centuries, the literate bourgeoisie of those provinces, in their struggle against the hereditary ruler from Spain, in fact took it from their reading in Greek and Latin, adapting it in their own fashion. It was appropriate to the cultivated speech of the Prior of the Cordeliers ("My godson, Monsieur de Withem, one of the Patriots . . ."). The adjective *Belgic* is another word that caused me problems. Some readers who were not very *au courant* about the history of the language believed it was born around 1830, when, instead, it died, to be replaced by the word *Belgian*, and was rather awkwardly reincarnated in the proper name of a then new nation. Certain worn-out words can serve, like a nail, to fix a date, and their use is then legitimate: when Zeno emerges from his meditation on time and space and recalls that at that moment he is lying on a corner of Belgic soil, that adjective takes him back into the sixteenth century.

Ancient man, at least when he belonged to that small minority of cultivated minds which hides from us all the other, illiterate minds of the time, tended, on principle, to rationalize the irrational and to move from the particular and concrete to the general and essential. With certain specific exceptions, of course: in history, as I've already said, Suetonius; in art, the carvers of Roman portrait busts. The great minds of the sixteenth century, again with certain specific exceptions, individualize and particularize. One has only to compare an anecdote of Plutarch with its retelling by Montaigne to be convinced of this. The language of *The Abyss* was obliged to take account of this specificity in practically every line. The vocabulary of the sixteenth century is, happily, close enough to our own so that a specific word for the designation of a specific object only occasionally causes the modern reader a semantic shock. Had I wished to render every detail of every incident of Hadrian's life, I should have had cautiously to get round the words *tric-*

linium, quadriga, and *sella curulis,* partly to avoid any pe-
dantry, but especially to leave antiquity its aspect of unencumbered space—which aspect is patently false, and yet at
the same time is also partially true if one recalls that the
Near East or even Italy has always tended toward a simple
way of life, even in ostentation. In *The Abyss,* on the contrary, every word referring to an object, as well as the object
itself, is often (for how much longer?) familiar enough to
us to become, when Zeno's meditation demands it, suddenly *unfamiliar*—which an object or a word belonging to
a civilization too far back from ours could not achieve. For
the painters of the northern Renaissance, objects form a
whole with the personage represented and, sometimes,
overwhelming him, acquire a disquieting sort of life of their
own; so also in *The Abyss,* the objects, and accordingly the
words that designate them, become the expression of a certain rapport or the sign of a certain submission to necessity.
Thus, to choose from among many examples: the bowl of
soup that Zeno takes in the refectory of the convent after
a sleepless night at the bedside of the prior, the blade less
than two inches long which will open the way to death for
him, and the nightshirt he uses to stuff up the space between
the door and the floor of his prison so that the guard will
not see blood on the floor of the corridor. Each precise word
became a part of the conditioning of the characters, that
conditioning which most of them submit to passively, but
which some, like Zeno, explore and, to a certain extent,
manage to rid themselves of, even at the cost of their lives.

What I've said about words designating deeds and things
should also be said about words which characterize individuals. In *Memoirs of Hadrian,* even had the book been
written in a "polyphonic" style (and this is a good reason
why it wasn't), we would have heard almost no specific
differences between the language of Arrian, Attianus, Cha-
brias, and Hadrian himself; the variants would be ones of
temperament (the tone of Trajan, for example, would some-

times have had to be more jovial, sometimes more imperious than that of Hadrian); the intellectual orientations—Stoicism for one, Pythagorianism for another, Pyrrhonism for a third—would at most have been perceived as subtle nuances: taken together, these intelligent men belong to an all-embracing culture and, at least at their level of society, speak more or less the same language. The tonal differences among the characters of *The Abyss* form a series of opposing angles—in part, to be sure, because time has not eroded to the same extent the conflict of their opinions, the consequences of which still affect us; in part, above all, because sixteen centuries of often badly formed thoughts, or thoughts that shouldn't have been formed at all, have dug indelible furrows into men's minds. Rightly or wrongly, the ancient world seems to us less scarred. The three ecclesiastics introduced into *The Abyss* do not speak the same language, and none of them *knows* completely, or at least doesn't *use* completely, that of Zeno. The philosopher and the canon appear to converse, yet almost none of the underlying ideas of the former reaches into the man of the Church, who is nevertheless judicious in his fashion; and nothing of the experience of the unfaithful monks really penetrates his legalistic and theological mind, even though he is their judge: they might just as well have lived in another time and another world. The bishop's impersonal tone is nothing other than that of the schools of his day: it teaches us nothing about the man. The very spontaneous language of the Prior exists on at least three levels: that of the former statesman who is well informed about public affairs; that of the director of conscience and the father superior, who is strict and austere; and that of the man of prayer. Zeno, with a clearly warranted prudence or a defiance of the Church the Prior represents (combined with a tenderness for who he *is*), sometimes feigns not to understand his poignant confidences; but it is no doubt also true that the profound plainsong of charity in the words of his pious protector eludes him, at least at first. In contrast, the Prior penetrates the mind of his interlocutor more than Zeno realizes, yet he voluntarily places a zone of silence between his friend's overly audacious thoughts and his own ("Pray do not insinuate a thing which I do not wish to hear"). The captain Henry Maximilian, a man with an open mind, who has had the experience of certain humanist teachings and is bound to Zeno by shared memories of childhood, *hears* the words the philosopher speaks; beyond a certain point, though, he no longer follows them. Princes and merchants confine themselves to their professional vocabulary of merchants and princes.

Zeno's language is made out of successive formations. The oldest is the Flemish of the street, the servants' hall, of the more or less clandestine encounters with workmen, which comes back to the surface during the last years he spends in Bruges. The French spoken in his home is already a language of culture; it is also the language of the books he writes and of his conversations with the Captain and the Prior of the Cordeliers. But the German, Italian, Spanish, and even Arabic from his years of wandering vie for position with this French. The Latin from his scholastic education unfailingly returns to his lips; if he thinks with these various tools of language, he reasons in Latin, or at least with the aid of the logical principles which come to him from that language: that is why I planted a bit of that Latin, which has no connections with that of the humanists, here and there in his talk, like so many signposts. The scientific language, with its mathematical metaphors as they would have been formulated in the seventeenth century, is clearly not yet his own; the language of experiments, which is his, also belongs to the artisans with whom he works and the sick people he takes care of, German in Lübeck, Flemish in Bruges. One of his distractions in prison will be to contrive an ideal language for himself which is free from any constraint except that of logic. In the chapter entitled "The

Abyss," where he finds himself on the borders of the inarticulate and the ineffable, words and even concepts become silent; the differing states of consciousness are translated into the metaphors of alchemy, in which float all the recurrent myths of humanity.

I believe I came to this spontaneity of language, which is beyond thought or speech, only toward the end of the first section of the book. With very few exceptions (the most notable of which is perhaps the day spent by Zeno in the forest of Houthuist), the first hundred pages preserve the tone of a chronicle; the few conversations are composed of what the author assumes her characters would have said in those circumstances: they do not spontaneously flow from their lips. The account of the festivities at Dranoutre interrupted by the arrival of the weavers is composed contrapuntally, and each voice enters only for its appropriate part, too measured to be anything more than a sonorous tag. The conversation between Zeno and Wiwine is written to the tune of a ballad, but it's hard for me to know whether that was because I was satisfied with that stylized form and that rather superficial level, or whether the young girl herself could not have spoken otherwise, or even the young Zeno, who surrenders to the game. In any case, it doesn't seem to me that complete freedom of language is achieved until the moment when Zeno, matured and already beginning to age, meets his comrade Henry Maximilian again at Innsbruck. From that moment until the end of the book, I had the impression I was a bit farther away from the reconstruction of life in the sixteenth century and a bit closer to that life itself.

1972

EXAMPLES OF SPOKEN LANGUAGE
WHICH HAS NOT BEEN SUBJECTED
TO LITERARY REARRANGEMENT

Official report of the trial of Campanella, 1597–1601

I. *Report of a spy*

A certain Francesco Tartaglia, detained for twelve days in the Castel Nuovo of Naples by order of the Royal Councilor, Don Giovanni Sánchez de Luna, several times heard Fra Tommaso Campanella and Fra Pietro Ponzio speaking with each other. In particular, on the night of April 14, Tartaglia and two prison guards, Martínez and Onofrio, heard the following:

Fra Pietro called four times to Fra Tommaso, saying:

Fra P.: O Fra Tommaso, Fra Tommaso, Fra Tommaso, O Tommaso, don't you hear me, my beloved friend?

Fra T.: Hello! Hello!

Fra P.: O, dear heart, how are you? Take courage, for the messenger is coming tomorrow, and we shall learn something.

Fra T.: O Fra Pietro, can't you arrange to get this door opened so that we can sleep together? That would be such happiness!

Fra P.: Would that God might make it possible for me to give the guards ten ducats and you, my beloved friend, ten kisses every hour! I distributed your sonnets throughout Naples, and I know them all by heart. There's nothing I'd rather do than read something of yours.

Fra T.: I plan to give some copies to the messenger.

Fra P.: Oh yes, dear heart, but do me the grace to give me some first, for me and my brother Ferrante, and then make some for the messenger.

Fra T.: Go to sleep now. Good night.

[*Signed*: Tartaglia]

[In another hand]

Fra T.: Have you any news of your little brother and your godfather?

Fra P.: They've put them with the laymen, with Gioseppo Grillo and Francesco Antonio Olivieri.

Fra T.: That's where your brother is?

Fra P.: Ferrante is with that bunch of laymen.

Fra T.: Oh, what a pity! Who knows what will become of poor little Francesco Antonio d'Oliviero . . .

Fra P.: Now you see . . . Have you written much today?

Fra T.: Yes, quite a bit.

Fra P.: Martínez isn't in the Castel, and the captain has called for Onofrio. We can speak freely.

Fra T.: You don't know the Spanish!

Fra P.: I know them well enough, *and* their crimes!

Fra T.: Do you know if Thomas Assarus is free?

Fra P.: I know nothing. Ask someone on the floor above.

Fra T.: That's not possible. Fra Pietro, tomorrow I'll try to slip you a note containing what I daren't say aloud. I hear someone.

Fra P.: God save us from them. Speak in Latin: they are ignorant and don't understand it.

[They are silent for a moment.]

Fra P.: There's no one. They wouldn't come without a torch.

Fra T.: Do you have any light?

Fra P.: No, none at all.

Fra T.: I see light. Let's go to sleep.

Fra P.: Let's go to sleep.

II. *Minutes of a torture session undergone by Campanella*

a) July 18, 1600

The accused: I feel terrible.

They tell him they are going to torture him again.

The same: Please, no! What do you want of me? I'm dead.
They ask him why he will not answer their questions.
The same: I can't . . . Aaaah, aaaah, aaaah! Assholes! My whole
    body hurts, brother . . . Let me down . . . Have you
    no pity?
They ask him why he does not tell the truth.
The same: I can't stand it anymore. Brother, I'm pissing. [And he
    begins to piss.]
For a while he is silent. Then he says:
The same: I'm shitting in my pants.
Then he is silent. They ask him to speak.
The same: I can't.
They tell him to beg the Lord Judges for mercy.
The same: Let me shit . . . My God, I'm dying!
They ask him if his dinner was good.
The same: I can't stand it anymore.
They ask him the name of the Commissioner of the Holy Office
who arrested him.
The same: Let me go to sleep, Fra Tomaso . . .
They ask him who Fra Tomaso is.
The same: Fra Tomaso is me.
They take him down and lead him back to prison.

b) Session of June 4–5, 1601, in the presence of two bishops and
an apostolic pronotary

They tell him he'll be cruelly treated if he continues to play the
fool.
He answers:
The accused: Ten white horses . . .
Several more impertinent answers. They tie him to the rack.
The same: Tie me tight . . . You're crippling me. Aaaah! O my
    God!
They tell him to be reasonable.
The same: I've done nothing to you . . . Let me go, I'm a saint!

> . . . *Sanctus sum, miserere* . . . Aaaah! My God . . . I
> am dead, my dear heart! Dead! . . . Oh, they're tight-
> ening my hands . . . Oh, I haven't done anything.
> Listen! . . .

And he continues to cry out, saying over and over:

The same: Aaaah!

And he suffers the torture, saying:

> *The same*: Oh, where are the soldiers who helped me? . . . Please
> come . . . Oh, I'm dying . . . Help me! . . . I'm shit-
> ting . . .

They tell him not to play the fool.

> *The same*: Let me go . . . Don't kill me . . . I'll give you a dozen
> carlins . . . I've done nothing!

They tell him not to play the fool. Then, as they were tying his
feet, he said:

> *The same*: Oh, they're killing me . . .

And when he hears the trumpet calls from the boats in the port
of Castel Nuovo, he says:

> *The same*: Blow! Blow! They've killed me!

They tell him not to pretend, and he remains silent, his head
bent down over his chest, for an hour.

They tell him they will let him down if he agrees to talk, but he
says only:

> *The same*: No . . . I'm pissing . . .

He asked to get down, and was let down, and said:

> *The same*: I want to shit.

And they took him to the latrines. And then he was interrogated
again by the Lord Judges, and he says:

> *The same*: My name is Friar Tommaso Campanella.

They ask him where he was born and how old he is. He does
not answer. The Lord Judges order him to be put back on the
rack. They put him back and arrange him on it. He says:

> *The same*: Oh, you're killing me!

They order him to answer and not go to sleep. He says:

> *The same*: Please be seated . . . Please be seated . . . A chair . . .
> Be quiet . . . Be quiet . . .

They ask him where he was born and how old he is, and he says:
The same: Help!
And he is silent.
They tell him to stop playing the fool, and he keeps silent.
He bows his head and says:
The same: Alas! Alas!
And when the first hour of the night had passed, they again asked him where he was born and how old he was, and he says to the Lord Judges:
The same: Don't do this! I am your brother!
And he is silent.
And they tell him not to play the fool, and he says:
The same: Give me something to drink!
And they give him a drink, and he shouts out:
The same: Help! . . . O joy!
And the second hour of the night passed, and they tell him not to play the fool, and he says:
The same: Do not kill me, brother!
And they ask him if he is a priest or a layman, and he replies with many impertinences, and says:
The same: I am a Dominican . . . I say Mass
And he lists many members of his family, and asks for a drink.
The same: Give me some wine!
And they give him wine, and he says:
The same: Oh, I hurt everywhere . . .
And he says nothing more the rest of the night, but suffered on, with the candles lit. And daybreak came, and they opened the windows and put out the candles. And he still kept silent. And they tell him not to play the fool, and he says:
The same: Oh, I'm dying . . . I'm dying . . .
And they asked him why he was arrested, and he says:
The same: I'm dead, I can't stand it anymore, O God!
And they tell him not to play the fool, and he says:
The same: I'm dying.
And the Lord Judges command that the torture be stayed, and that he be placed in a chair, and that was done, and as he was

sitting down he says that he wants to piss, and they take him to the latrines near the torture chamber. And the third hour came, and they were about to put him back on the rack, and he says:
The same: Wait, brothers!
And once on the rack, he says nothing more, and he stayed there, suffering, calm, and silent. Then he asked that they lift his feet up a bit because they hurt badly, and they did it, and he rested quietly. And the Lord Judges asked him if he wished to sleep, and he says:
The same: Oh, yes!
And they tell him that if he will speak they will let him sleep as much as he wants, and he says nothing.

.   .   .

[Confrontation with another accused]

And then they let him get down to eat and drink and go to the latrines, which took an hour, and they put him back on the rack, and he says:
The same: What do you want of me?
And he appeared not to feel the pain any longer, and he said nothing.
And the Lord Judges, hearing that he had asked for some eggs to eat, had him given three on a plate, and when they asked him if he wanted anything to drink, he said yes, and they gave him some wine, and the Lord Judges said that they would give him more if he would speak, and they announced to him that they were going to start the torture again, and he says:
The same: Leave me alone!
And they ask him why he is so preoccupied with his body, and he answers:
The same: The soul is immortal.
And all the time he kept repeating:
The same: I'm dying, I'm dying . . .
And the Lord Judges ordered him to be taken down, cleaned up,

dressed, and taken back to his cell, and the torture had lasted thirty-six hours.

[*Signed*] Johannes Camillus Pretiotus
Notary in Ecclesiastical Trials and Transactions of the Archiepiscopal Tribunal of Naples

.   .   .

And a warden charged with taking the prisoner back and consigning him to the jailers of the Castel heard him say as they were crossing the royal hall:
The same: And they thought I'd be asshole enough to talk.

Official reports 345, 402, 404, 395
(Luigi Amabile, *Fra Tommaso Campanella*, Naples, 1882)

4

THAT MIGHTY
SCULPTOR, TIME

On the day when a statue is finished, its life, in a certain sense, begins. The first phase, in which it has been brought, by means of the sculptor's efforts, out of the block of stone into human shape, is over; a second phase, stretching across the course of centuries, through alternating phases of adoration, admiration, love, hatred, and indifference, and successive degrees of erosion and attrition, will bit by bit return it to the state of unformed mineral mass out of which its sculptor had taken it.

It goes without saying that we do not possess a single Greek statue in the state in which its contemporaries knew it: we can barely discern, here and there on the hair of a Kore or a Kouros of the sixth century, the traces of reddish color, like palest henna, which attest to their pristine character of painted statues alive with the intense, almost terrifying life of mannequins and idols which also happen to be masterpieces of art. Those hard objects fashioned in imitation of the forms of organic life have, in their own way, undergone the equivalent of fatigue, age, and unhappiness. They have changed in the way time changes us. The maltreatment of Christians or barbarians, the conditions under which they have spent their centuries of aban-

donment underground until discovery has given them back
to us, the sagacious or ill-advised restorations from which
they have benefited or suffered, the accumulation of dirt
and the true or false patina—everything, including the atmospheric conditions of the museums in which they are
today imprisoned, leaves its mark on their bodies of metal
or stone.

Some of these alterations are sublime. To that beauty
imposed by the human brain, by an epoch, or by a particular
form of society, they add an involuntary beauty, associated
with the hazards of history, which is the result of natural
causes and of time. Statues so thoroughly shattered that out
of the debris a new work of art is born: a naked foot un-
forgettably resting on a stone; a candid hand; a bent knee
which contains all the speed of the footrace; a torso which
has no face to prevent us from loving it; a breast or genitals
in which we recognize more fully than ever the form of a
fruit or a flower; a profile in which beauty survives with a
complete absence of human or divine anecdote; a bust with
eroded features, halfway between a portrait and a death's-
head. This blurred body is like a block of stone rough-hewn
by the waves; that mutilated fragment hardly differs from
a stone or a pebble washed up on some Aegean beach. Yet
the expert does not hesitate: a line which is worn away, a
curve which is lost here and reemerges there can only result
from a human hand, a Greek hand, which labored in one
specific spot during one specific century. The entire man
is there—his intelligent collaboration with the universe, his
struggle against it, and that final defeat in which the mind
and the matter which supported him perish almost at the
same time. What he intended affirms itself forever in the
ruin of things.

Those statues which have been exposed to the sea-wind
have the whiteness and porosity of a crumbling block of
salt; others, like the lions of Delos, have ceased to be animal
effigies and have become blanched fossils, bones in the sunlight at the edge of the sea. The gods of the Parthenon,

affected by the atmosphere of London, little by little are turning into cadavers and ghosts. The statues reconstituted and repatinated by eighteenth-century restorers, made to harmonize with the shimmering parquets and polished mirrors of papal or princely palaces, have an air of pomp and elegance which is not antique but evocative, rather, of the festivities at which they were present, marble gods retouched according to the taste of the period standing side by side with ephemeral gods of flesh. Even their fig leaves clothe them like the dress of that time. Lesser works which people have not taken the trouble to shelter in galleries or in pavilions made for them, quietly abandoned beneath a plane tree or beside a fountain, ultimately acquire the majesty or the languor of a tree or a plant: that shaggy faun is a moss-covered tree trunk; this bending nymph is indistinguishable from the woodbine that embraces her.

Still others owe their beauty to human violence: the push toppling them from their pedestals or the iconoclast's hammer has made them what they are. The classical work of art is thus infused with pathos; the mutilated gods have the air of martyrs. Sometimes, the erosion of the elements and the brutality of man unite to create an unwonted appearance which belongs to no school or time: headless and armless, separated from her recently discovered hand, worn away by all the squalls of the Sporades, the Victory of Samothrace has become not so much woman as pure sea-wind and sky. One bogus aspect of modern art comes from these involuntary transformations of ancient art: the Psyche in the Museo Nazionale of Naples with her skull cut cleanly off, horizontally cloven, has the appearance of a Rodin; a decapitated torso turning on its base recalls a Despiau or a Maillol. What our sculptors today imitate by willful abstraction, and, moreover, with the help of cunning artifice, is there intimately bound to the fate of the statue itself. Each wound helps us to reconstruct a crime and sometimes even to discover its causes.

That emperor's face received a hammer blow on a certain

day of revolt or was rechiseled to serve for his successor. A rock thrown by a Christian castrated that god or broke his nose. Out of greed, someone extracted the eyes of precious stone from this divine head, thus leaving it with the cast of a blind man. A German mercenary boasted that he had tumbled that colossus with one shove of his shoulders during a night of pillage. Sometimes the Barbarians are responsible, sometimes the Crusaders, sometimes the Turks; sometimes the lansquenets of Charles V and sometimes the soldiers of Napoleon; and Stendhal was later moved to tears at the sight of the Hermaphrodite with a broken foot. A world of violence turns about these calm forms.

Our ancestors restored statues; we remove from them their false noses and prosthetic devices; our descendants will, in turn, no doubt do something else. Our present attitude represents both a gain and a loss. The need to refashion a complete statue with artificial members resulted in part from the naïve desire to possess and exhibit an object in perfect condition, which is inherent to all ages because of the simple vanity of the owners. But that taste for excessive restoration which all great collectors from the time of the Renaissance down to our own day have possessed surely arises from profounder causes than ignorance, convention, and the vulgar bias in favor of a fair copy. Our forebears—perhaps more human than we and with different sensibilities, at least in the domain of art, from which they hardly demanded more than pleasurable sensations—found it hard to put up with mutilated masterpieces and with marks of violence and death on gods of stone. The great lovers of antiquities restored out of piety. Out of piety, we undo what they did. But possibly we are more accustomed to ruins and wounds. We are suspicious of any continuity of taste or of human spirit which would permit Thorvaldsen to repair Praxiteles. We more easily accept that this beauty, so remote from us and lodged in museums rather than in our homes, should be a dead beauty or a beauty made of fragments. And, finally, our sense of the pathetic is gratified by these bruises; our predilection for abstract art causes us to like those lacunae and fractures which tend to neutralize the forceful human element in this statuary. Of all the changes caused by time, none affects statues more than the shifts of taste in their admirers.

A form of transformation more striking than any other is that undergone by statues which have fallen to the bottom of the sea. The vessels which carried work commissioned from a sculptor from one port to another, the galleys into which the Roman conquerors crammed their Greek loot to transport it to Rome, or else to take it along with them to Constantinople when Rome became less sure, sometimes went down with all hands. Some of those shipwrecked bronzes, fished up in good condition like a drowned man revived in time, have acquired from their subaqueous sojourn nothing more than a beautiful greenish patina—as, for example, the Ephebe of Marathon or those two powerful athletes from Erice found recently. Fragile marble statues, on the other hand, emerge gnawed or eaten away, corroded, decorated with baroque volutes sculpted by the caprice of the tides, or encrusted with shells like those boxes we bought at the seaside in our childhood. The forms and gestures the sculptor gave them proved to be only a brief episode between their incalculable duration as rock in the bosom of the mountain and their long existence as stone lying at the bottom of the sea. They have passed through this decomposition without pain, through this loss without death, through this survival without resurrection, as does all matter freed to obey its own laws. They no longer belong to us. Like that corpse in the most beautiful and haunting of Shakespeare's songs, they have suffered a sea-change into something rich and strange. That Neptune, a good workshop copy intended to decorate the quay of a small town whose fishermen would offer him their first catch, has de-

scended now to the realm of Neptune. This Celestial Venus, or Venus of the Crossways, has become the Aphrodite
of the Sea.

1954
1982

5

ON A DREAM
OF DÜRER'S

One is unlikely to come upon many authentic dreams in texts from another time; I mean dreams that the dreamer himself has hastily noted down upon awakening. Some splendid dreams recorded by Leonardo in his *Notebooks* bear a curious resemblance to his drawings and paintings, but they give rather the impression of some oneiric experience extended into the state of waking or half waking than of a dream properly speaking. The poignant dreams of Dante in the *Vita Nuova* and the great allegorical dreams of Cardano are also located within this intermediary zone—between dream, dream perceived upon awakening, and *visio intellectualis*—experienced by numerous poets, painters, and philosophers from the Middle Ages to the Renaissance, but into which modern man rarely ventures or, when he does stray into it, does so unprepared and without a guide.

Yet we possess from a man of the sixteenth century the extraordinary account of a dream which is nothing but a dream, and, what is more, accompanied by a supporting sketch. It is found in Dürer's *Journal*. Here is the account the artist, scarcely awakened, has left of his dream:

In the night between Wednesday and Thursday after Pentecost [June 7–8, 1525], I saw in a dream what this sketch displays: a number of

Dürer, *The Vision*, Kunsthistorisches Museum, Vienna

waterspouts falling from the sky. The first struck the earth some four leagues off: the blow and its noise were terrifying, and the entire region was inundated. I was so frightened I woke up. Then other waterspouts fell in appalling violence and number, some striking the earth farther off, some nearer. And they fell from such a height that they all seemed to fall in slow motion. But when the first waterspout was close to the earth, its fall became so rapid and was accompanied by such a noise and such a roaring wind that I woke up, trembling in every limb, and took a long time to get over it. So that, once I had arisen, I painted the above picture. God makes everything turn out for the best.

This dream is striking for its complete lack of symbols. A German critic sees in it the effect on Dürer of the upheaval caused by the Reformation; but that's his theory. A psychoanalyst would suppose that the great painter was obsessed by water; but that remains to be proved. Water is not very dominant in the paintings and engravings of Dürer, and when it does appear, it is never catastrophic. One thinks of the peaceful Inn, with its limpidity that fills us today with nostalgia, in which the walls of Innsbruck are reflected, or of the calm Adige lapping the walls of Trent, or of that darker, almost fiercely solitary pond in a clearing which also possesses an imperturbable tranquillity. Not only is the image of violent water almost totally absent from his work, but even this inundation seen in a dream doesn't at all correspond to the biblical sort of *Flood* in which mankind's fear and despair dramatically predominate. The sole rain which falls in his *Apocalypse*, engraved some fifteen years earlier, consists of huge drops of water falling from a cloud in which there appears a dragon with a lamb's head, and this is a minor detail. What is surprising, moreover, is how little cosmic these images from the Book of Revelation are in Dürer, and perhaps also in Saint John before him, despite the showers of stars, the flames, and the clouds—which are symbolic configurations of the merely human drama.

In his oneiric sketch, on the contrary, the visionary is a realist, and it is of a cosmic drama that he is the spectator. He has the precision of a physicist. At the shock of the first waterspout, he tried to measure how far away he was from the point of impact, and then to judge the others in comparison with it. He noted the apparent slowness, then the accelerating, dizzying speed of these downpourings from far above. What is rare in a dream, so far as I am aware, is that he *felt* the percussive impact and *heard* the thunder of the falling water. One curious detail is that he says he was awakened by the shock of the first cataract, leaving us uncertain as to whether this awakening was part of his dream or whether he fell back asleep at once and was plunged again into the same cataclysm. In either case, the effect is one of a natural disaster perceived without reference to any human concept as it might have been refracted in a block of crystal without any human eye's beholding it. The terror which shakes the sleeper is, to be sure, a human reaction, yet an animal might just as well have experienced it, and this physical perturbation is very similar to that of an earthquake.

Look closely at the sketch, or rather the wash drawing, which depicts this dream. The enormous waterspout like a mass of blue-black clouds involuntarily makes us think today of an atomic mushroom; but we must reject such an overly facile prefiguration. The landscape seems crushed in advance by the dirty blue floods that fall vertically from the sky; the earth and the water which has already fallen are mixed together in a muddy brown and a murky gray: if one were obliged to identify this place with some spot on earth, one would think of the Lombard plain—which Dürer crossed more than once—because of the few scattered trees which are vaguely present in that atmosphere of catastrophe yet which one feels were planted and perhaps pollarded by the hand of man. Far off, made small by the distance, hardly perceptible at first glance, some brownish structures huddle on the edge of a bay, apparently ready to turn back into clay. What is about to be destroyed is not especially beautiful.

I repeat: there is no religious symbol in the margin, no avenging angels signifying God's wrath, no alchemical symbol of the "forces which descend," which would be pointless in the presence of the terrible gravitation of the cataracts. Nor is there any humanistic meditation, tragic as in Michelangelo or melancholy as it will be in Poussin, in the face of our greatness and smallness when confronted with the raging universe. Unless, perhaps, the best aspects of humanism are contained within this capacity, even in a dream and at the heart of a kind of ontological anguish, to persist in taking the measure of things.

The narrative itself ends on a pious formula, placed there by a man awakened from his dream. It reminds us, had we been tempted to forget, that Dürer was a Christian—twice a Christian, as it were, inasmuch as he was the heir and sublime interpreter of medieval piety on the one hand, and a citizen of Nuremberg, on the other, who at the end of his life hailed the Reformation. It can be variously interpreted as a quasi-mechanical propitiatory formula, as the more or less sincere assertion of an optimism based on divine benevolence (as inconclusive as some casual sign of the cross), or, on the contrary, as a very conscious submission to the order of things, which is always characteristic of every authentically religious great spirit. Marcus Aurelius accepting what the universe wills, Lao-tse in harmony with the void and Confucius with Heaven. But to say "on the contrary" is too much. We imagine that simple faith and impersonal adherence are somehow joined within those depths of human nature where the principle of contradiction does not enter. As such, this Christian mantra no doubt helped Dürer to emerge unscathed from his dreadful dream.

1977

6

THE NOBILITY
OF FAILURE

The reputation of the great English scholar of Japan, Ivan Morris, is well established. His *The World of the Shining Prince: Court Life in Ancient Japan** combines an exactitude of sociological information with the most perfect literary tact; his annotated translation of the poetess Sei Shōnagon, the contemporary and rival of the author of *Genji*, almost completely recaptures for us the refinements of the Heian period and its rather impressionistic poetic style. *The Nobility of Failure* is the last great book of this scholar whose premature death is a loss for all lovers of Japanese history and literature.

In the preface to this book, which is dedicated to the memory of Yukio Mishima and was partly inspired by that great and strange writer, Ivan Morris tells us that Mishima, who was his friend despite their often divergent views, reproached him for being overly interested in the glorious Heian period (eighth to eleventh centuries A.D.), a sort of ravishing Belle Epoque which in Japan preceded a harsh Middle Ages, and for thereby neglecting the more savage

* The book concerns the time of the protagonist of *The Tale of Genji* by Murasaki Shikibu (eleventh century).

aspects of the race, those of the time of the samurai and the civil wars. In *The Sea of Fertility*, the tetralogy which concludes his work, Mishima himself seems to have taken account of this dichotomy: the hero of the first of the four novels, a young Japanese from the years around 1910, has, with his taste for love and for tears, all the refinement of a prince from the Heian period. The young hero of the second novel (set in 1932), a murderous rebel who kills himself, thinks and acts quite otherwise, like a samurai out of the past. In *The Nobility of Failure*, Ivan Morris also directs his attention toward these heroic and violent aspects of the Japanese spirit.

But opposing and complementary aspects are never as distinct as one might believe. Whether they are medieval or almost contemporary, the vanquished and the suicides whom Ivan Morris depicts for us are distinguished from their Occidental counterparts by a specifically Japanese characteristic: the poetic contemplation of nature at the moment of death. Whether it is the melancholy Prince Yamato Takeru of the fourth century A.D. or Ōnishi in 1945 or the great Saigō, champion of the oppressed peasants in the nineteenth century, they all die with poetic refinement.

O lone pine tree!
O my brother!

sighs in death Prince Yamato Takeru, who had been sent to perish in yet unconquered regions on a desolate plain at the foot of a mountain by his father the emperor, who employed this classic method to get rid of a son who had become an encumbrance. The statesman Michizane (tenth century), whom the benevolent government of the Heian period was content to sentence with exile but who ended up dying of homesickness the way those courtiers excluded from Versailles under Louis XIV languished away, evokes in his grief the trees of the garden he has left behind:

If the east wind blows this way,
O blossoms on the plum tree,
Send your fragrance to me!
Always be mindful of the Spring,
Even though your master is no longer there!

In the nineteenth century, the illustrious Saigō, about to disembowel himself after having fomented a peasant revolt in vain, seeing disaster approach from afar, turns to his beloved nature:

I do not mind the bitter cold of winter;
What fills my heart with fear is the cold hearts of men . . .
I know that my end is near:
What joy to die like the tinted leaves that fall in Tatsuta
Before they have been spoiled by autumn rains!

In the twentieth century, the young kamikazes, the pilots of suicide planes, also bade a poetic farewell to life before taking off with no chance of return. Thus, in 1945, a twenty-two-year-old pilot:

If only we might fall
Like cherry blossoms in the Spring—
So pure and radiant!

Several days after Hiroshima, the aged admiral Ōnishi, who was responsible for the whole kamikaze saga, performed seppuku* in his turn, and, after an atrocious death agony which lasted several hours (he had refused the traditional coup de grâce), left a last poem beside his bed:

Refreshed and clear, the moon now shines
After the fearful storm . . .

---

* Term of Chinese origin used in preference to the more vulgar *hara-kiri*.

The exquisite delicacy of *Genji* and samurai heroism come together in these brief poems which issue from the same source: an awareness of the tragic transience of life which leads both to poetry and to sacrifice. One can hardly imagine Robespierre or Napoleon, or even the "aces" of the First World War, comparing themselves to a lone pine tree or to falling blossoms as they departed this world. To be sure, these poems of despair and agony are traditional in Japan and are thus, if you will, conventional. Yet so lively a convention remains a force: their sense of identity with the universe perhaps explains in part the amazing ease with which these men of violent action die.

Without following Ivan Morris's stories one by one, let us at least isolate their dominant strains. His early heroes, almost legendary young princes, victims of their fathers' hatred or their uncles' malevolence, remind us of the melancholy Prince Hamlet. Later, when imperial power had faded and was replaced by that mighty, virtually hereditary dictatorship, the shogunate, the same conflicts burst forth within a different group. The unhappy Yoshitsune, brother of the great head of state Yoritomo, triumphed over his brother in popular sympathy if not in history. One cannot read the story of his short life, taken by Morris from the chroniclers of the twelfth century, without also thinking of those Noh and Kabuki dramas which recount his tragic legend. Nothing is lacking: the shining victories of the young hero who annihilates the enemy clan and brings victory to his brother; the hatred of the new shogun for his brother, on whose head a price is put; the flight of the rebel prince disguised as a mendicant monk, encountering loyalty in some places and treachery in others; and finally, the ritual suicide of a man who is determined to die free. Yoshitsune has his Ophelia, less unstable than Hamlet's: the dancing girl Shizuka, one of his mistresses, whose infant son Yoritomo killed and whom afterwards, when she had recovered from her confinement, he forced to dance before the whole court; but merely by the beauty of her gestures the young woman succeeds in making her audience weep for the banished prince. *Get thee to a nunnery!* This advice, not taken by Ophelia, was followed by Shizuka, who took the habit in a Buddhist convent.

Yoshitsune has his Horatio also, who is at the same time his Frère Jean des Entommeures and his Sancho Panza: Benkei, the huge monk whom he disarmed in a duel with the blow of a fan and who, raised bit by bit to the stature of a true hero, defends the banished prince, sometimes by force and sometimes by guile, and who finally dies, pierced by a rain of arrows on the threshold of the casemate in which Yoshitsune has taken refuge, in order to allow his master to commit suicide in peace. According to Morris, the captivating figure of Yoshitsune left its mark forever on Japanese sensibility—which was, it must be admitted, already oriented in this direction. Even today, the word *hōganbiiki*, "sympathy with the lieutenant" (Yoshitsune began life as his brother's lieutenant), continues to signify pity for the defeated and love of lost causes.

One of the advantages of such a bird's eye view of Japanese history is that it prevents us from attaching to these men from another world our own sorts of labels, whether laudatory or condemnatory. From the fifteenth century, in any case, the Japanese hero doomed to failure is above all a samurai, member of an impoverished, aristocratic military class, vassal of the powerful daimyos who ostentatiously display themselves at the court of Kamakura or of Edo, while the emperor, reduced to a symbol, pursues at Kyoto his existence as high priest and master of ceremonies of a civilization already a thousand years old. This protectorship of the emperor was nothing new: as early as the Heian period, the members of the clan in power took the sinecures for themselves, married the emperor to a girl from their circle, then agreed to force him to abdicate, leaving an infant in the cradle who, after an extended regency, would in turn abdicate at about the age of thirty. The rebel and "loyalist" samurai dreamed of a time when the imperial benevolence would descend from on high directly to the people—as it had, they said, in mythic times—without the intermediary of the shogun and his daimyos. "Reactionaries" in the eyes of the shogun establishment, the samurai are also "radicals" who make common cause with the oppressed populace.

But what is so striking is that the refinements and comforts of that Japan (and in this respect Japan is not alone) are derived, almost perforce, from the subjection of a half-starved peasantry. The immense fortunes of the princes and grand functionaries are calculated in thousands of bushels of rice. Theoretically, every farmer legally possessed a few acres for his own use; in fact, and increasingly, the peasants worked (as a bitter saying had it) thirty-five days a month for the state. The exactions and brutalities of the Treasury are scarcely discernible in the literature of the Heian period, which is a court literature: for Murasaki and Sei Shōnagon, the populace consists of domestic servants, porters, workmen come to labor within the confines of the palace, and a few rustics seen on the road from afar; the last two types were astonishing for their gross manner of speaking and eating. From the Middle Ages onward, there are many testimonials about the methods of collecting taxes: decapitation, crucifixion, or the dire "dance of Mino," reserved for insolvent farmers, who were dressed in a cape of rice straw drenched with oil which was set afire at nightfall so that the victim, who leapt about convulsively, could be seen from far off—an object lesson for recalcitrant farmers in other villages. In the bad years, endemic shortage of food turned into famine. The situation worsened in the eighteenth century with the rise of big commerce and the voluntary or forced exodus of the peasants to the city.

This situation was to persist until the end of the shogunate in 1868 and, in a slightly different form—that of an industrial civilization—until well into the twentieth century. In

1933, Isao, the hero of a novel by Mishima I have already mentioned, launches a terrorist attack against the members of the industrial establishment, who, in his view, shield the venerated emperor from the misery of the people. This fanatic "fascist," who slays a millionaire financier with his own hands (a crime rarely committed by Western fascists), is motivated by the economic crises of the thirties—inflation, the import of foreign rice which ruined the small farmers, the sad, commonplace stories of farm girls sold to brothels in the cities and of young soldiers sent into Manchuria, happy to die in order to spare their families one more useless mouth to feed.*

In the face of such constant abuses, it is not surprising that the samurai evoked by Morris should have taken as their motto: "Save the People!" All of them ended in heroic defeat. The most extraordinary is doubtless Amakusa Shirō, a young, sixteen-year-old samurai converted to Christianity, who in 1637 raised a battle flag of revolt with a eucharistic emblem on it and put himself at the head of forty thousand insurgent peasants. Pursued by the troops of the shogun, he ended by taking refuge with some twelve thousand partisans, all Christians like himself, within the ancient fortress of Hara at the southernmost extremity of Japan; they held out there for several months before they were massacred to the last man. That was the end of the Christian episode in the Land of the Rising Sun, and the defeated peasantry paid dearly for that incredible venture. After that, the leaders of the peasant class are lettered samurai, deeply imbued with neo-Confucian doctrines which accept thought only insofar as it ends in action, and who consider, like William the Silent in Europe, that "one need not hope in order to undertake." Ōshio Heihachirō, who had sold the

---

* It is striking that two other of the most remarkable twentieth-century novels of Japan, *The Cannery Boat* by Takiji Kobayashi (1928) and *Narayama* by Fukazawa Shichiro (1956), are based on the theme of poverty and hunger.

fifty thousand volumes of his library in order to aid the starving, ended in 1837 by putting himself at the head of a revolution and burning the shops of the merchants of Osaka, which he considered he had a right to do since they were exploiters of the people. After an atrocious repression had decimated his partisans, he committed suicide and persuaded his son to do the same.

Twenty years later, the shogunate fell into ruin following the "opening" of Japan by Commodore Perry, and the "loyalists" restored the emperor, who abandoned Kyoto for Tokyo; but, for all that, the poverty of the peasants wasn't alleviated. The huge Saigō the Great, a Tolstoyan type of character who, sent off to an unsalubrious island because of his rebellion, tried to fight against the working conditions there on the sugar plantations, was for a time a member of the new government under the Emperor Meiji, but finally resigned when he perceived that only the men and not the mistaken methods of the past had been changed. In 1877, quitting his voluntary exile as a literate country gentleman, this giant, who went barefoot even in the palace and who had refused the salary of his position "because he didn't need it to live," rose against the corruption of the regime he had helped to establish. His army of twenty-five thousand men was cut to pieces by the regular troops, and he performed seppuku, following the example of Ōshio. "A man of the right," exclaim those who see in the man who gave his cohorts the imperial chrysanthemum for their emblem one of the members of the anti-shogunate restoration. "A man of the left," pronounce those who depict him as "ready to slay the police of Tokyo" and as treating his former colleagues as "the worst criminals on earth." In fact, he was neither one nor the other, but both. Like Ōshio's, his revolt exists above all in a philosophical and moral sphere. "Revere heaven; love humanity," he said, and for him humanity meant the poor. "Civilization is the guardian of justice." Many hollow idealists have proclaimed similar slogans. Ōshio and Saigō signed theirs with their blood. In his chapter on the kamikaze, Morris's work breaks new ground. Together with the remarkable work of Richard Minear, *Victors' Justice*, which deals with the trials of the war criminals in Tokyo, his is the only book I know which presents a picture of the war in the Pacific and its aftermath from the enemy's point of view as well. At least until Hiroshima, that war took place in a period when the United States still had a clear conscience. The surprise attack on Pearl Harbor certainly caused indignation, yet no one had thought to assign responsibility for the series of intrigues, takeovers, and white or yellow encroachments which had taken place in this vast region for more than a century. The maltreatment suffered by prisoners in the Japanese camps rightly caused horror, but no one understood that to be a prisoner was traditionally a dishonor in Japan, where every man would have preferred death—which explains, even if it doesn't absolve, their brutal treatment of enemy captives. The bravura of the Marines was celebrated, as it should have been; but it took Morris's book to show many American readers the extremes of heroism to which an army accustomed to winning, and the nationals of a country never until then invaded, were carried in defeat. The mass suicides, from the Aleutian Islands to Guadalcanal, were nowhere more spectacular than on Saipan, where three thousand men armed with bayonets and sticks rushed against the enemy artillery, helping their wounded, bandaged comrades, fresh from the hospital, to take part in this appalling attack; encircled, the soldiers, rather than surrender, knelt in rows to be decapitated by their officers, who in turn performed seppuku. Entire families jumped off cliffs. So that, of the thirty-two thousand people who three days before lived on the island, at most a thousand (and only a handful of soldiers among them) survived.

It is against that background of inadequate information that the kamikaze period was portrayed for the average

American; it was its absurdity that was emphasized above all. One has to follow, in Morris's book, the adventures of those thousands of young volunteers, mostly students, only a few dozen of whom, at most, were to know the shame of surviving (as the result of chance or of some unexpected countercommand). It is the foreseen, calculated choice of death in the kamikaze forces which is so fascinating, despite or possibly because of its complete uselessness. Only a few small American units were destroyed by the suicide planes. The mighty battleships were hardly damaged or were, at worst, repaired in a few days: when the alert was over, the Marines hosed down the decks on which the "pure cherry blossoms" had crashed in bloody flames. Occasionally, the bomb didn't go off, or the plane brought down by a barrage exploded some distance from the targeted ship. "Forward, even in defeat, always forward!"—the ancient samurai spirit had its last effulgence there, at least in our time; for it would be imprudent to make predictions, if not about tomorrow, at least about the day after tomorrow. That those fires have continued to burn under the ashes is proved by the admonishing and protesting suicide of Mishima, which was equally planned and calculated in its smallest details, and by the more recent suicide of a young actor (whose name escapes me) who, employing the kamikaze technique, took an airplane and crashed it into the roof of the house of a well-known person involved in one of the Lockheed scandals. Certainly, faced with those thousands of young men who died for a cause already lost, it is impossible not to ask oneself if they would not have served better by continuing to live, and if they might have kept Japan from that easy acceptance of a foreign yoke which so quickly followed its war frenzy, from that industrial imperialism which is as greedy and shortsighted as the imperialism of the war strategists, and from the aftermath of pollution which has perhaps fouled forever a country for whom the idea of the purity and holiness of nature had until then been quintessential. One may well ask. The violent heroes are not always the heroes of peace.

There is only one point on which one might dispute Morris. He is fond of claiming that love for those defeated in a lost cause is an eminently Japanese thing, and that our Western world offers no examples of it—the only defeated we honor being, according to him, those whose cause finally triumphs. But, on the contrary, love of lost causes and respect for those who die for them seem to me to belong to all countries and all ages. Few escapades are as absurd as that of Gordon at Khartoum, but Gordon is a hero of nineteenth-century British history. Rochejacquelein and "le Gars" in Balzac's *Les Chouans* are certainly defeated, and their cause with them, unless one considers the few years' reigns of Louis XVIII and Charles X as a triumph: they speak no less forcefully to our imagination. The same is true of the Girondins and those sent to the guillotine on 9 Thermidor, whose political views one can hardly say triumphed but who count among the great human myths of the French Revolution. And it is probably much more Waterloo and Saint Helena than Wagram which made Napoleon such a beloved subject for the poets of the nineteenth century. I once caused a Roman emperor whose story I evoked to say that a moment comes when "life, for every man, is an accepted defeat." We all know that, and it is what makes us admire so much those who have consciously chosen defeat and who sometimes have achieved it early on. There is a bit of "sympathy with the lieutenant" in all our hearts.

1980

7

FUR-BEARING
ANIMALS

I've been asked to collaborate on a collection entitled *Angry Women*. I dislike that title: I approve of indignation, which in our day finds only too many occasions for exercising itself, but I can't say that I approve of anger, that tiny individual irruption which disqualifies, blinds, and leaves one short of breath. Nor do I like the fact that this collection is exclusively limited to women writers. Let's not build again compartments for women only.

Yet, if I write these few lines, it's because I imagine, rightly or wrongly, that a book written by women will be read by women, and it's to them especially that the following protest is addressed. Whenever—generally in a dentist's or doctor's waiting room—I happen to leaf through fashion magazines, especially those deluxe ones on glossy paper, I go quickly past (trying not to see them, as if they were pornographic photos) those full-page advertisements on which all the seductions of Technicolor have been lavished. I mean those in which female individuals parade themselves in sumptuous fur wraps. These young people, whom any eye endowed with double vision sees dripping with blood, wear the spoils of creatures who once breathed, ate, slept, sought partners for their amorous sport, loved their young, sometimes so much as to get themselves killed in order to protect them, and died, as Villon would have said, "to pain"—that is, in pain, as we all shall; but these creatures died a death savagely inflicted by us.

What is worse, many of these pelts come from animals whose species, antedating ours by thousands of years, is about to become extinct and will disappear, if we don't look to it, long before the charming people who wear the pelts will have reached the age of wrinkles. In less than a generation, the raw material of these status symbols (as they are called and should not be) will be not only "unfindable" or "unobtainable"; it simply will no longer exist. To all of us who give our time and money (though never enough of either) to try to save the diversity and beauty of the world, this slaughter is repugnant. I'm not unaware, of course, that these young ladies are models: they dress themselves in these scalps because it's their job, just as they also get themselves up in a bra and panties called, in honor of an atomic explosion (another jolly association of ideas), a bikini. These innocent girls doing their job (who yet would doubtless very much like to own one of these costly wraps) nonetheless represent a whole race of women—those who devour these pictures with their eyes, dreaming of a luxury which is inaccessible to them, and those who possess these sorts of spoils and exhibit them like some proof of wealth or of social rank, of sexual or career success, or even as some accessory they can count on to make them beautiful and charming.

Finally, let's strip these women of their last shred of an excuse. Today, even if they live in Greenland rather than in Paris, they have no need of these skins to warm their own. There is enough good wool, high-quality yarn, clothing which holds or radiates heat, so that they are not obliged to metamorphose themselves into furry animals the way females had to in prehistoric times.

But I am taking it out on women: the trappers are men; the hunters are men; the furriers are men, too. The man who is proud to walk into a restaurant in the company of a woman bristling with animal skins is very much a man, even if not necessarily a Homo sapiens. In this area, as in so many others, the sexes enjoy equality.

1976

8

MIRROR-GAMES
AND
WILL-O'-THE-
WISPS

You think you are dreaming, and you are remem-
bering . . .

BACHELARD

. . . that mind for which every object in the world
was a phenomenon or a sign.

M . Y .

The minutes of the trial for witchcraft of a peasant who
was condemned to death at Bailleul in 1649, at the bottom
of which two of my ancestors have placed their marks, have
come down to us in bundles of documents containing more
or less similar cases. This is thanks to copies which were
made of them before whatever managed to survive the fires
of the sixteenth and seventeenth centuries in this small
town's archives had finally gone up in smoke during the
wars of our time. I learned about them only several months
ago, in the course of research for a book I am currently
writing. But around 1937, at the time when I was already
once again thinking of that work abandoned along the way
which was eventually to become *The Abyss*, I happened to
examine, pencil in hand, a volume devoted to the history
of the magistrature under the Ancien Régime. An incomplete note indicates to me that I found there, or thought I
had found there, mention of another, later affair. At the
beginning of the eighteenth century, Michel-Ignace Cleene-
werck, the purchaser of Crayencour, had, in his function
as magistrate of Bailleul, interrogated about some unre-
corded misdeed a seminarian who was traveling with
gypsies.

My incomplete note gave neither the title nor the author, both of which I had forgot. The copy I used had disappeared, along with a good number of other books in my possession, during the confusions of 1939–45. Since then, I had forced myself to read a number of works about the court proceedings of former days which were published before the time in question, without ever finding again those lines whose imprint, so to speak, had stayed in my memory—on the left, at the bottom of the page. In the end, I began to suspect that I had invented them, and along with them the incident itself, or at least that I had added the name of my forebear Michel-Ignace to some text about an anonymous magistrate or one with another name. With this whole matter it was the same as it was with the name Zeno, a fairly common name in ancient Flanders, which I still believe I remember having read at around the age of twenty in the rough draft of a genealogy of my family I was shown at that time. The genealogy has since reappeared, but the name Zeno doesn't figure in it.

In any case, whether read or imagined, these facts played their role in the creation of *The Abyss*. I immediately seized upon the name Zeno, which I liked because, although it was fairly frequently used in this region in the times of faith, honoring a bishop saint of Verona, it was also the name of two ancient philosophers, the subtle Eleatic, put to death, it is said, by a tyrant, and the austere Stoic who appears to have killed himself, as was often done in his sect. As for the incident of wandering about with gypsies, it still figures on a list I made in 1965 when, close to finishing *The Abyss*, I enumerated elements which might be included in the composition of the final chapters. In the end, I didn't use it.

On the whole, my memory is very reliable. To say that memory and imagination feed each other is to stay within the most general données of the problem. If there was indeed a memory, if these facts are found in some archival

document that I may one day or another put my hands on,
I should like to know how it was that they so immediately
imposed themselves upon me as living, assimilable ideas
over which my mind has never ceased to play. If it was in
fact fabulation, then it has to be explained why I contrived
these images, and these images in particular.

It is strange to hold in one's imagination or one's memory
(in one or the other, or in one and the other) the wet clay
of a reality which perhaps isn't one. It is equally strange to
see, as also happens, history catch up with us and have the
invented person or incident turn out to be real. In 1964, as
I was working on the third section of *The Abyss* during a
stay in Central Europe, I saw in my mind's eye, in the
church of the Franciscans in Salzburg, the character of the
Prior of the Cordeliers appear, who was utterly unforeseen
until that moment and whose introduction partly changed
the direction and meaning of the work. I had to supply this
holy man with a first and last name. For a last name, I
chose Berlaimont, a well-known family, many of whose
members played rather important roles in the Low Countries in the sixteenth century; for a first name, Jean-Louis,
the simplicity of which seemed fitting for the Prior. To a
great degree, the first and last names were chosen for their
consonance in French: amidst the throng of my Flemish
characters, I wanted to depict in Jean-Louis de Berlaimont,
the former courtier of Charles V, a man of international
culture, whose exquisite French "was restful to Zeno's ear
after the sound of the thick Flemish speech."

In the course of the story, the Prior, who had entered
holy orders as a widower, alludes with sadness to his son,
a young officer of the Duke of Alva, a man of war through
whom this man of peace vaguely feels he has his "share in
evil." Several chapters further on, the course of my tale
allowed me to encounter this young Berlaimont so devoid
of his father's spirituality, in the company of the Duke. As
he ate with his fine white teeth off the silver plate of his

hosts, the rich Ligres, he indiscreetly made some remarks to them about the financial difficulties of the army. I needed a first name for this slightly blundering, handsome lad; I decided on Lancelot, a name sometimes used at the time, though not very frequently, because it evoked so well the atmosphere of those poetic and artificially prolonged Middle Ages, their tourneys, their orders and romances of chivalry, their caparisoned steeds and dress armor, in which the future Prior, the young Jean-Louis de Berlaimont, had been engulfed at the court of the youthful Charles V at the moment when his son was born.

In 1971, three years after the publication of *The Abyss*, finding myself for a second time in Namur in order to visit a place near which my mother spent her childhood, I decided to look carefully at the archaeological museum of the town, which had been in a state of reorganization during my first visit, so that I had been able to see only a few cases of Belgo–Roman jewelry that had been moved to another site. The old mansion in which the museum is located today is very handsome. In the hall where the stairway is located, I happened upon a tombstone. The label informed me that it came from the Church of the Minorite Friars (i.e., the Cordeliers) in Namur, today called Notre Dame. Beneath the coat of arms was the following inscription:

Within this coffin lie the remains of
MESSIRE LANCELOT DE BERLAIMONT
Count of Meghem, Baron of Bauraing, Seigneur of Dorimont,
Agimont, Hardaing, Desperlecheg, Governor of Charlemont,
Captain of forty men-at-arms
of His Majesty's guard,
and Colonel of the Bavarian Regiment,
who died XI June 1578

It is not only the first and last names which "coincided" with those of my character. The rank in the army and the dates are also appropriate. A colonel of a Bavarian regiment killed in the siege of Namur in 1578, virtually at the same time as Don Juan of Austria, could have been, and even should have been, one of the young lieutenants of the Duke of Alva ten years earlier. What I had thought was a mask modeled by my hands was suddenly filled with a living substance.*

I do not note the preceding facts with the intention of proving anything whatsoever, and I should be terribly embarrassed to have to define what they might prove. On a rational level alone, they are easily explained and dismissed. It is natural that, among the hundreds and thousands of pages read, our memory no longer knows very well if some particular lines have been remembered as they are, or, on the contrary, if they have been refashioned by our imagination, or, even more likely, invented in the way the imagination invents—that is to say, by combining details and names taken from elsewhere. Nor is it extraordinary that very precise calculations in the spheres of history and literature, undertaken with a view to giving an imaginary character the greatest possible plausibility, could end up by bumping into, as if by chance, a person who actually existed. What continues to cause us to dream, however, is the number and intensity of obscure impulses which direct us in this way towards one name, one fact, one character rather than another. There we enter into a pathless forest.

.   .   .

I find this same play of the fortuitous and the fanciful in another, still more inconclusive form in my initial work on another book, which is still only a sketch, or, more accu-

---

* I must add a note, however. Ten years later I found in a book which came from my father's library a chronicle of the sixteenth century containing the name of a certain Lancelot de Berlaimont. It is plausible that I could have read or leafed through this book between my fifteenth and twentieth years and recalled it many years later.

rately, a project. Between the publication of *Memoirs of Hadrian* and *The Abyss*, I began in a small way to prepare for a work I had provisionally entitled *Three Elizabeths*. The main section was to have been about Saint Elizabeth of Hungary, one of the most moving of those chosen for the calendar of saints, the study of whom leads us far in various directions and deep into obscure problems. There is the problem of her spiritual election, which makes this young girl a chosen being from her infancy in the bosom of that royal and brutal milieu whence she came; there is that of the incomprehension and hatred which surround saints, from the hostility of Elizabeth's in-laws to the jeers of the common people who saw the young woman, once elegantly garbed in her long sleeves of samite, going through the streets in rags, obsessed with caring for the poor—not to mention the obtuse harshness of her confessor, who was partly responsible for her death and about whom she appears to have learned to make judgments. There is the problem of the harmonization, so difficult to achieve and even more difficult to express, of sensuality and sanctity, resolved on the spot by the young saint when, upon quitting her prayers, she "threw herself laughing" onto the bed where her young, handsome husband awaited her. And that of the rapports between poetry and mystical genius, so apparent in this child whose birth was announced to the Minnesingers by the appearance of a star and who died one November day, at the age of twenty-four, while sitting in the embrasure of her window listening to the banal yet marvelous song of a little bird. Not to mention not so much the problem as the mysterious depths of the perpetually gaping, shining abyss of charity.

I was also interested in the relations of the most spontaneous of saints with the State and Church of her time, and in a certain number of somber and luminous presences whose movement one senses around her almost as much as one does around that other ingenuous figure, Joan of Arc.

The seraphic flame of Francis of Assisi, whose example and teachings inspired her without her ever having encountered him on her journey through life; the dark authority of the Inquisitor Conrad de Marburg, flaying with his whip the delicate skin of his penitent and casting upon her, whether she knew and approved of it or not, the reflections of the trials of heretics and the burning stakes; the icy radiance of the Emperor Frederick II, who almost married this young and pious relative and who, if he had, would doubtless have relegated her to his "harem of Gomorrah," along with his other spouses—the same godless prince who, with motives more political than religious, would later preside over her canonization. Those cords that bind a person to her time, those blemishes and gleams of light which the century casts on her, and the secret powers of genius or of sanctity which occasionally deliver her from them—all that would have composed a spiritual symphony (as Saint Bernard might have put it) around Elizabeth, a spiritual symphony not without dissonances.

Three Elizabeths . . . It's as foils, or at least as contrasts to the saint, that I would have placed two other women, born in other times but belonging to the same regions of Central Europe, more or less set on feudal or princely summits, and possibly possessing, through the complicated matter of lineages, a drop or two of the same blood. One was to have been Elizabeth of Austria, the empress, so celebrated and perhaps overrated by poets at the beginning of the century, a phantom of sadness, pride, and beauty, whom a melancholy narcissism seems to have imprisoned in some dismal hall of mirrors until the end, so withdrawn from the world and from life that she was not even aware that her assassin, Luccheni, was stabbing her to death. Although we lack the mirror before which she delivered those long monologues we can only conjecture about, at least those two objects which were placed upon her coffin the day of her funeral are fitting symbols for this goddess: her riding crop and the fan she employed to ward off the stares directed at her. They accompany her into eternity, like Saint Elizabeth's rags and bouquet of roses. The third, more or less a contemporary of Shakespeare's women and as shrouded in infamy as a human being can be, was to have been Elizabeth Báthory, a somewhat less sensitive, less refined Gilles de Rais, who appears to have achieved a sort of imbecility in crime. These three women would have indicated the paths which lead to salvation or perdition, or that crossroad which leads to neither but only to the limbo of poetry and dream.

Elizabeth of Hungary was inspired by Francis of Assisi; Elizabeth of Austria, by Heinrich Heine. It appears that just as Gilles de Rais's madness was aggravated by that nobleman's association with an evil magician, so Elizabeth Báthory accelerated her utter disintegration by surrendering to acts of sorcery with the village ghouls, whom one imagines as having somewhat the features of those filthy witches of Hans Baldung. Those crones, who also served her as bawds and as co-executioners, called up a certain devil, Isten, lord of cats,* to serve their mistress, and Elizabeth wore around her neck a talisman containing an invocation to eighty hellish cats who were meant to bite the hearts of her enemies. It ended with what always happens to all talismans of witchcraft, which, we are assured, turn against their owners. Elizabeth lost hers, and a bad copy she had had made was used in evidence against her at her conviction.

Right after the condemnation of this shrew, as soon as she had been immured for the rest of her existence in a chamber of a vacated dungeon, the village pastor (her branch of the Báthory family was Lutheran) climbed the slope of the château to pray in front of the brick wall that had been

---

* In Hungarian, *Isten* means God. Thus, Elizabeth Báthory invoked a cat-god, or, more precisely, set up as a god the Satan worshipped by these witches in one of the customary animal symbols he adopted in the Middle Ages.

erected. Ill-received by the prisoner, he was also troubled by a frightful caterwauling of cats, who leapt onto his head. Yet when they climbed to the floor above, neither he nor his churchwarden found anything up there but an empty room. Unrepentant to the end, did Elizabeth, during the three years she spent in that chamber, believe she sometimes heard a scampering about and a meowing on the deserted floors and in the courtyards? We don't know, because we know nothing more about her, except that a villager carrying keys and a basket of provisions climbed every day up to the château (at the four corners of which flew black standards to indicate that a death sentence was being carried out there), opened the successive doors, mounted the stairs of the tower, and passed the food through a grille to the prisoner. One small detail, which is moving because it is so human: she complained about the food, which at first was only bread and water. A son-in-law of the murderess gave some money so that she would get a cooked meal every day until she died. This woman, who was guilty of hundreds of sadistic murders, was, in her everyday life, evidently a mother-in-law kind enough to have received this act of charity from one of her sons-in-law.

As I went along, the title of my project changed to *Elizabeth, or Charity*. I realized that the central problem—or the central flame—was there, and that the melancholy Elizabeth and the bloody Elizabeth would occupy only a few dark corners of my work. Then some other undertakings, more essential for me, got in the way of this one: first, *The Abyss*, then *Souvenirs Pieux*, and then its companion piece, *Archives du Nord*, which I am working on at the moment. *Elizabeth, or Charity* will no doubt remain one unrealized project among a half dozen or so others, one of those works about which I often think but which I shall possibly not have the time, energy, or even, when the time comes, the desire to write. There are so many other things to be done, among which the most important are not necessarily books.

Yet the subject interested me sufficiently that in 1964 I decided to include in a trip I made to Central Europe some of the places where these three women had lived. I traveled to Europe aboard the *Báthory*, which I can't really consider a coincidence: it was the only ship which went directly to Scandinavia and Poland, and it owes its name to the illustrious Polish king, Stephen Báthory, not to the Ilse Koch of the Renaissance. I was obliged to abandon part of my itinerary connected with these three women: a lack of time, complications over visas, and, above all, other priorities got in the way. Nevertheless, in Salzburg I made a point of going to see once more, in the handsome park of Hellbrunn, the white statue of Elizabeth of Austria; yet I was preoccupied above all with memories of Paracelsus, with the little stone bench in front of an old shop under whose overhanging roof I caused Zeno to sit, dead tired after crossing a mountain pass in the snow, and also with that period of self-communion in the church of the Franciscans which I mentioned earlier. All that formed a mute accompaniment to the music of Mozart, without which one can't imagine Salzburg. In Vienna, a woman who drove me around and treated me like a tourist continually misidentified for me, in various squares and parks, the statues, both ugly and handsome, we came upon: according to her, that of Elizabeth of Austria represented Maria Theresa, the wife of Joseph II. When I expressed some doubts, she became red with anger. I concluded that the primary schools of the Austrian state teach history even less well than ours. In Bratislava—that is, Pressburg—I took the trouble to go to see the heavy baroque castle, high above the city, which replaces the medieval fortress where Saint Elizabeth was born. I could no longer find the old, gray, aristocratic town in which I caused the protagonist of *Alexis* to dwell for several seasons. The only thing that remained unchanged was the turbulent course of the Danube, even more dammed up and polluted than it had been in the thirteenth century, or even at the beginning of the twentieth.

In Slovakia, not far from Piestany, I went to see the castle in which Elizabeth the murderess perpetrated her crimes and arrogantly endured her punishment until her solitary death, "without light or crucifix," one stormy night in 1614. The slope that led up from the village was steep. The solitude which reigned there was that of ruins and no longer that of a condemned habitation. At the foot of the walls, a small vegetable garden, no doubt belonging to the absent guard, was beginning to show its green above the earth. It was doubtless in such a garden that the dogs of that other time had unearthed the remains of Elizabeth's victims, hidden in haste under the loose, worked earth. There, sorrel and lettuce put forth, on that warm morning, their almost divine cleanness.

On the other side of the postern, nothing survived but the eviscerated tower of a dungeon, the bare area of an empty courtyard, and trenches broken by time and adorned with creeping vegetation. I went up to a low wall. It did not look out over vertiginous, romantic chasms but rather over the village with its descending roofs, the smiling plain (which seemed almost Italian), and, here and there, the rigid, black hills the last spurs of the Carpathian Mountains—bristling with pines as in the landscapes of Altdorfer. Something moved. A huge black cat dashed, cursing, from under the branches, leapt across the courtyard, and disappeared on the side opposite the ravine.

I'm not suggesting that this cat was under the dominion of the devil Isten. It was surely the tomcat of the guard, trying for the little young lives of tiny birds hidden in some nest under the leaves. Nonetheless, of the several dozen medieval castles whose ruins I have visited, Báthorygrad is the only one where I've seen a black cat suddenly appear the moment I entered, acting as if he owned the place.

The second little coincidence is even stranger, although its context is terribly banal. Upon returning to my island in Maine, I went to the excellent public library in Bangor on the mainland, some eighty kilometers from where I live.

I rarely go to Bangor, a substantial provincial town without much charm which stands on the plain where that immense forest of oaks stood into which Champlain ventured to meet some Indian chiefs at more or less the same period when the black standards of justice floated over the castle of Báthory. I go even more rarely to the town's public library, since a nearby seminary possesses another one, less complete but more selective, and has the additional advantage of a charming reading room. On that particular day, I went up to the high counter to deposit in the appropriate box my slips requesting some books I no longer recall. A book which had been returned by its reader and was not yet put back on the shelves by the attendant lay open on the counter. I glanced at it, as I always do at any printed text I come upon. It was the only work in English I know of which mentions Elizabeth Báthory, a collection of essays by William Seabrook, who has done better work, listing at random several dozen criminal cases and tales of black magic, true or false. Only a couple of paragraphs are devoted to this particular witch: but the book was open at that page.

Far be it from me to claim that an evil spirit came that day, or several days before, from Slovakia to cause a frequenter of the Bangor library to choose this volume out of several hundred thousand others, and then to return it opened to this page an instant before my arrival. Like everything which to a greater or lesser extent touches upon unexplored regions, this faint sign, assuming it was one, was so inconsequential as to be ridiculous. There is utterly no necessity to assume that the intervention of obscure forces placed before my eyes a mediocre work I had leafed through at the time of its publication some twenty years earlier. Nevertheless, to establish the calculation of the probabilities necessary to produce this small coincidence, one would have to play with figures containing a whole row of zeros. At such moments, everything happens as if the world about us were located in one sole magnetic field, or as if it were constituted in each of its parts of some metal which is a good conductor. When one thinks about it, that would be more or less the structure of the universe of Chinese divination, such as Jung elucidates it in his preface to the *Li-King*.

It will be noted that these slight coincidences are all associated with the worst of my three models. Neither Elizabeth of Hungary nor Elizabeth of Austria made any sign —unless one is obliged to interpret as such the incident of the angry Viennese driver and sees there an SOS from a ghost already half buried in oblivion. Saints and empresses apparently have more dignity than witches. However, for Elizabeth of Austria the vital current passed much earlier. Once I knew an old Maltese coachman on Corfu who in his youth had been a groom of the empress. I didn't much like the bric-a-brac of the Achilleon, even though the passionate admiration of Elizabeth for Achilles strangely resembles, across the centuries, that expressed in the letter of Arrian to Hadrian known as *The Periplus of the Black Sea*; but the fact is, I had not yet read it at that time. I didn't much like that royal amazon who drank a glass of warm blood from the slaughterhouses every morning in order to preserve her beauty; Báthory herself couldn't have done better. But the affectionate accounts of the old coachman presented the disarming portrait of a German woman, no longer young, who knew all about grooming, who was capable of scolding her grooms or, on the other hand, of smiling on them while keeping her distance, and who never tired of asking them to sing her Corfiot ballads. In the house of some people I knew, a glass case exhibiting a single long white glove, the melancholy spoils of a dead hand, touched somewhat more closely upon magic. Elizabeth had dropped it one day, during one of her interminable and slightly demented excursions through the countryside, when she had come into the house to ask for a drink of water. An aura of human warmth seemed to hover over it.

The encounter with Elizabeth of Hungary goes even further back. As far as mysteries are concerned, she had only that of her infancy. The villages of French Flanders in my time still had a taste for religious processions which, despite their faded gilt and tarnished cheap finery, were somewhat reminiscent of the splendid religious processions in Spain. In place of the grandiose effigies of Seville, the sacred figures there were represented in flesh and blood, generally by children. Between my fourth and eighth years, each Corpus Christi morning, dressed in a gown of tulle and a cape of orange-red velvet into whose lining a bouquet of artificial roses had been sewn for fear that I might otherwise drop them along the way, I trotted along the sole street of the village of Saint-Jans-Capelle and the roads of Mont-Noir, stumbling slightly in my tiny white ankle boots, which didn't really go with my medieval garb. I knew very little about the figure I represented: never having been near any sick people, I failed to see what Elizabeth's merit was in having taken care of them; ignorant of hunger, both in myself and in others, I wasn't moved by the gift of bread to the starving. On the other hand, the metamorphosis of that same bread into roses seemed to me quite natural; for nothing astonishes a small child.

Someone might say that my interest in the little saint of ancient Hungary began there. I would claim as much myself. But the explanation doesn't stand up. It doesn't explain at all the supremely mysterious character of our rapports with the characters in our books, which is the subject I've attempted to investigate here. Shortly after my last impersonation of Elizabeth of Hungary, I was sent to a children's dance dressed up as a little drummer boy from the armies of the Empire. All my equipment seemed quite authentic, including the drumsticks and buttons engraved with eagles. Yet that masquerade has not caused me to want to write the history of Napoleon.

1975

9

ON SOME
EROTIC AND
MYSTIC THEMES
OF THE *GITA-*
GOVINDA

India possesses great erotic myths: Parvati and Shiva united in an embrace which lasts thousands of divine years, the product of which would cause the destruction of the world; Shiva seducing the wives of the heretical anchorites, who call up monsters to avenge themselves and manage only to furnish God with new attributes and new adornments; the cut-off head of Kali placed on the body of a low-class prostitute, the divine joined to what is thought to be unspeakably filthy. Of all these myths, doubtless the most beautiful, the most charged with devotional and mystic significance, the one that best conveys not only the emotions of the senses but also those of the heart, is the descent of Krishna amongst the shepherdesses in the forest. The celestial shepherd wanders about in the forest, charming beasts, demons, and women with the sound of his flute. The Gopis, delicate milkmaids, gather around him in the thickets where their cattle are grazing. The god, who is everywhere, simultaneously satisfies a thousand beloveds; each of them (if one may amend here the sense of a celebrated verse) has him for herself alone, and each of them possesses him completely. This phallic festival is a symbol of the marriage of the soul with God.

We find ourselves here at one of the great junctions of myth. This god in the woods, around whom prowl lascivious girls and who dispenses to them at once both a bodily and a mystic inebriation, is Dionysus; this musician who calms the frightened animals is Orpheus. This shepherd who satisfies the human soul's need for love is the Good Shepherd. But Orpheus on the banks of the raging Strymon dies for having scorned the wild desire of the Bacchantes; he leads his Maenads into complete animal abandon, in a world haunted by the ancient terrors of man; the Christian Good Shepherd is inseparable from the Cross. In contrast, there is nothing somber or tragic in the episode of Orpheus–Bacchus on the banks of the Ganges. The union of Krishna and the milkmaids is achieved in complete serenity, in the bosom of an Edenic innocence. The mystical forest of Vrindavana belongs to the world of the perennial pastoral. Venus in the stable with Anchises or in the glade with Adonis, Apollo tending the flocks out of love for Admetus, Tristan and Isolde in the *Minnegrotte*, Siegmund and Sieglinde listening to the murmurs of the spring night on the doorstep of their woodland cabin, Tess of the D'Urbervilles concealing her love in the milk house among the farm girls, and even the powdered figures out of eighteenth-century bergeries—all of these characters, immersed in a world that is both ideal and primitive, which at first glance appears factitious to us but which is no more so than any other dream of happiness, have Krishna and his ardent milkmaids as their distant prototypes.

It cannot be denied that Christianity has endeavored to lead the human soul back to a state of prepubertal innocence more imaginary than real and far removed from true childhood; that it has wanted, and in large part has achieved, a desacramentalization of the sensuous except in marriage, and that even there it has hedged it round with too many interdictions not to associate it forever with the notion of sin. But the evil comes from even further back than the

New Testament and the Church. Early on, Grecian intel-
lectualization and Roman rigorousness worked at a separation between the spirit and the flesh. The *Symposium*, the
noblest statement of Hellenic eroticism, is also the swansong
of pure pleasure: there the senses are already the slaves who
turn the millstone of the soul. Seneca has hardly less disdain
for the flesh than the medieval author of *De Contemptu mundi*.
Later, in Western Europe, the influence of superstitions
and barbarian codes came to reinforce the moralism of the
Church: Celts and Germans had burned or drowned illicit
lovers before the time of Christ. Later still, bourgeois re-
spectability, capitalist or totalitarian ideologies, the con-
structors of man the robot or of cybernetic man have
distrusted the free play of the senses no less than that of
the mind. For the European, sensual pleasure has, by turns,
been a more or less licit enjoyment yet always unworthy
of occupying for long the attention of a philosopher or a
citizen, a mystic rung in the knowledge of the soul, a shame-
ful satisfaction of the Beast who makes the Angels weep, a
sinful spice introduced into the holy broth of marriage, the
sublime crown of a unique love, a pleasant pastime, a soft
weakness, a subject for ribald jokes and the gymnastics
manual of Aretino's treatises. Everyone brings something
of his own to it: Sade his cold frenzy, Valmont his vanity,
Mme de Merteuil her taste for intrigue, the Freudians their
childhood complexes, the idealists their hypocrisy. In art,
even in those periods which were freest and most inclined
to sensuousness, painters and sculptors had to find alibis in
myth or legend in order to express the poetry of the senses,
or had to cover their lissom nudes with the protective var-
nish of aesthetic theory: Ingres himself would probably not
readily have admitted just how much pure voluptuousness
is in his *Turkish Bath*. In literature, it is more difficult than
one might imagine to find the depiction of sensual pleasure
enjoyed for its own self without the intervention of a phony
moral tacked on to reassure the reader and protect the au-

thor, a prefabricated disgust or abasement, an all-purpose scientific vulgarization, the thin smile or loud guffaw which permits everything. Nothing is more disorientating than to climb out from the depths of such confusion into the sacred naturalism of Hindu eroticism, to the notion of the divine experienced through the mediation of the physiological which impregnates the love games of the *Krishna Lali*.

A cheap sort of exoticism likes to exaggerate the permissiveness of Asia within the sensual realm. Yet the primitive codes of India are in fact hardly less rigorous than those of Leviticus: in their application, one is conscious of those eternal repressive forces which are the result of a superstitious terror of the sexual act, the jealousy or avarice of the leader or father who is inclined to turn the female troop into well-guarded livestock, the ignorance, the routine, the reasoning by analogy, the concern to reduce lustful sensuality to strict genital necessity, and, perhaps even more, man's curious instinct for arbitrarily complicating or simplifying that which is. The codes, indeed, are one thing; custom, another: this is especially true in the domain of the senses, where, more than elsewhere, the human creature seems to possess the ability to breathe easily in a zone comparable to profound depths, far below the changing surface of ideas, opinions, precepts, below even the level of the act as described in language or clearly perceived by the person who performs it. An amorous act traditionally condemned by Vedic scripture is freely depicted on the bas-reliefs of the temples of Khajuraho. It is no less true that everywhere, in every age, ambivalence rules in the matter of sexual morality, neither more nor less, in fact, than anywhere else, and that to the *yes* proclaimed on certain points there corresponds a *no* pronounced on certain others, as if a severity here should immediately compensate for a liberty taken there. India has hastened the marriage of its daughters in order not to have to reproach itself for a nubile woman's lack of satisfaction; but that same India has secluded its widows or delivered them to the flames. In the era when the Hindu sculptor represents so nonchalantly the frolics of Krishna and his milkmaids, the depictions of the Hindu hell threaten the lustful with torments as atrocious as those inflicted on carnal sinners by the devils in our cathedrals.

All the great religions born out of the soil of India have advocated asceticism. The Brahmin obsession with Being and the Buddhist obsession with Non-being both lead, in the Holy Man, to the same result, which is disdain for that which passes, changes, and terminates. The Hindu anchorite frees himself through asceticism; the sculptors of the Greco–Gandharan school have depicted Buddha leaving a voluptuously exhausted group of sleeping women. But his departure does not signify a flight from sin; his asceticism does not signify penitence any more than the ritual fear of impurity corresponds in any precise way to the Christian obsession with the sins of the flesh, which is nonetheless at its root. The detachment of the Hindu sage does not imply disgust, or Puritan censure, or hatred of debasement of the flesh. Indeed, in certain sects, as in certain heretical groups within the bosom of Christianity, the sexual act becomes for the mystic what it has never ceased to be in popular religion, one of the symbols and forms of the union with God. Absolute Being, the supreme Atman, contains within himself the act of love of the millions of people who make up our various worlds; the frenzied embraces of the gods of Tantric Buddhism are an accepted part of the Cycle of Things.

The more a strictly speaking Hindu sensibility developed in art, the more eroticism insinuated itself into the expression of forms. That eroticism which deliciously washes over the svelt nudes of the frecoes at Ajanta, swells the almost rococo curves of the river goddesses at Kailasa, and attains a dancing frenzy in the Shivaite statues of later epochs we also find in the bodies (now of more dumpy proportions) on the bas-reliefs of Khajuraho, of Aurangabad, of Maha-vilipuram, dedicated to the loves of Krishna and the milk-maids. Rounded, smooth, almost elastic flesh, dense with the soft density of honey flowing into honey. It seems as though, if sliced, these torsos would present a homogeneous, fleshy inside to the eye, like the pulp of some fruit. If cut off, these arms and legs would grow again like stalks or roots. Not blood but sap flows in them, or rather that sperm which the body of a Bodhisattva contained instead of blood. One isn't quite sure: that hand which touches a sexual organ, is it a hand or another sexual organ? Is it a knee or an elbow which bends around that naked thigh? Those mouths are suction cups; those noses rubbing against each other are drawn out into the shape of trunks. Those Gopis bend under the weight of their huge breasts, bowed like a bush sagging with its fruit. Impetuously, a girl with her legs drawn up, her heels together, leaps onto her god-lover like some monkey clinging to a tree trunk. This art of love confuses sexual characteristics almost as much as it does the characteristics of human and animal species: Krishna does not achieve the disquieting femininity of Shiva, that other inexhaustible husband, yet his hairstyles, his ornaments, and the rhythm of his shapes give rise to ambivalence if not to error. A fragment on which two mouths are joined or two bodies intertwined might be two Gopis embracing one another. It is only by his sexual organ that this thoroughly masculine god reveals himself as clearly masculine. At times, it even seems as though humor insinuates itself into these sacred scenes of Hindu statuary, the way it does into the work of our medieval image-makers, placing there the equivalent of that little repressed laugh which is, no less than the sigh, one of the sounds of love. But nowhere is there the nervous, almost unbearable twitching of certain erotic Japanese prints or the intelligent, almost purely intellectual statement of a Greek vase depicting an obscene subject. This profuse sen-suality floods out like a flat, spreading river.

My beloved was naked and, knowing my heart's desire,
Wore nothing but her sonorous jewels.
                                        —Baudelaire, "Les Bijoux"

Between the sixth and thirteenth centuries A.D., an India which had absorbed and partly eliminated the Greco–Gandharan lesson and had not yet felt the new Western influence brought in by Persian art expresses the amorous adventure of the "Blue God" in purely Hindu terms, by means of conventions that change so little that it is, at first glance, hard to distinguish a Gopi of the caves of Aurangabad from a Gopi of Khajuraho, who is her younger sister by about seven centuries. The intricate coiffures of their large dolls' heads remain perfectly in place, despite the acrobatics of love; their eyes, or rather their eyelids, are presented blank, with a blind cast that suggests the conventional highlight of theatrical makeup, as if it were less a question of opening the eyes to see than of closing them to swoon; the luxuriousness of the jewels enhances the nakedness of the flesh. Jewels, makeup, and hairstyling are everywhere a way of giving the nude the specific indication of a certain civilization and a certain time: this Krishna jingling with necklaces is a raja among his women; these Gopis possessed in that forest at the dawn of time are sacred dancers, their hips professionally dislocated by the postures of the dance; this bizarrely bent girl with a feather in her hand, staining the sole of her foot red, is performing an immemorial rite of the spouse's toilette. The very ubiquity of the divine embrace conveys the most secret desires of the harem at the hour of love. Those aesthetic or sensuous refinements which a European poet like Baudelaire tastes nostalgically, almost perversely, with a sensitivity which is all the more poignant inasmuch as it is experienced against the grain of his era, here belong to the banal, stylized language of pleasure. The uncustomary and the illicit, those two indispensable elements of all pornography, are completely irrelevant.

The epoch in which Hindu art and piety devoutly evoke the union of Krishna with his beloveds is roughly that in which, in the forests and over the heaths of medieval Europe, the ancient, peasant, pagan phallicism proscribed by the Church took refuge in the covens of witches. Those thousand beauties in the forest nestled against their wondrous lover and the old woman with pendulous dugs, riding her broom or clutching the diabolic ram, running into the Harz to copulate with Satan, are two virtually contemporaneous expressions of desire. The amatory flutterings of the Gopis can weary our eyes, and even our senses; but this frank eroticism saved India from our melancholy, diabolic arts.

Despite the merit of the translation (or perhaps because of it), it is difficult to judge fairly the literary qualities of the *Gita-Govinda*, that long lyrical recitative which, in the twelfth century A.D., the Bengali poet Jayadeva consecrated to the adventure of Krisha and the milkmaids—not because of his distance in time and space, but rather because this work, which, reeking of perfume, corresponds in an almost exaggerated way to the popular notion of Oriental love poetry, doesn't accord very well with the tastes or; possibly, with the literary assumptions of the European reader in this second half of the twentieth century. We have lost the habit of such luxuriance and languorousness. Of all the poetic literatures of Asia, that of India, from Kalidasa to Tagore, astonishes us with its abundance, its softness, its repetitive emphasis, its comparative indifference to the human act (submerged as it is in the universal flux), and the heady, mawkish savor of its romanticism. Jayadeva is no exception. His art has nothing of the primitive; it is learned, even literary; the Bengali poet finds himself in the same position with regard to the Sanscrit epic as the Alexandrians did with regard to Homer. Jayadeva takes up themes treated in the *Bhagavata Purana*, also a relatively recent text but one which is fed from a past already two thousand years old. They influence it even more than the Vedas themselves (in which the effects of the Aryan conquest or influence are felt), thus immersing the poem in the timeless substratum of an archaic India. In any case, Jayadeva emphasizes especially the romantic and voluptuous aspect of the myth: the motif of the pleasures given to the thousand milkmaids alternates with that of the laments of Radha, the abandoned one, until finally the god grants the tearful beauty her part of happiness. But the poetic universe of India is not one of individualization, or even of specific persons: while each of the thousand and three on Don Juan's list is still, however colorless, a discrete little creature more or less differentiated from the others, the thousand beloveds depicted by Jayadeva could be, simultaneously, the whole race of women and one single, identical woman; each Gopi in turn might be Radha.

Nor is this universe that of tragedy: jealousy is merely a passing disquiet; grief immediately dissolves into sensual enjoyment. The reader browsing through these moist images of rapturous nudity ends up thinking, despite himself, of that curious fantasy of preclassical French literature, that character in the *Dream of Francion* who wanders deliciously over a field of breasts. The fact is, the animal and vegetable analogy proliferates in Jayadeva as it does in the temple sculptures: Krishna is "the shining dancer who multiplies his members," "the tree trunk from which ramify branches of billing and cooing birds." Hair becomes creeping vines; arms, stalks; breasts, coconuts; vulvas, lotus flowers. Confused by a resemblance which is a cliché of the Hindu aesthetic, Krishna takes the trunk of a young elephant for the thigh of his beloved. What in Greece was expressed by metamorphosis is here expressed by a kind of delirious similarity. The *Gita-Govinda* is inseparable not only from those harmonics of allusions and literary resonances no poem can

do without, but especially from the entire Hindu civilization, from this culture at once more artificial than our own
and closer to the natural milieu out of which it comes—
from the ambiance of the small court in which these verses
were first written and recited in some pond-side pavilion,
from the women, the tame beasts, the sugared, peppery
taste of the sweetmeats, the haunting music, the facilities
offered for a desire both insatiable and immediately slaked,
from everything around Jayadeva that justified and nourished the mystical glorification of pleasure.

It is in the period which corresponds roughly to our
Middle Ages, and it is in Bengal in particular, that there
develops around the myth of Krisha this bhakti, this mystical devotion to ineffable Love, a notion, *mutatis mutandis*,
very close to certain forms of Christian sensibility which
recur through the centuries. What is more, in its reaction
against metaphysical speculation in favor of concrete piety,
medieval India seems to have experienced an evolution comparable to that which the Catholicism of the Counter-
Reformation was to experience several centuries later. The
swoonings of Sodoma's Saint Catherine or Bernini's Saint
Theresa, or the breasts of Mary Magdalene delicately veiled
by the penitent's disheveled hair, betray the same need to
combine sensual ecstasy with religious ecstasy that the
Hindu Gopis convey simply through sensuous pleasure. In
both cases, it is a desire to establish the most intimate union
between the adorer and the adored, to force the absolute,
the infinite, or the eternal to incarnate itself in a human face
not only inspiring love but also responding to love. With
Jayadeva, we are at once close to and far from that Krishna
who is the solar avatar of the Vedic scriptures, close to and
far from the sublime Lord whom the *Bhagavad Gita* causes
to express the most formidable ideas in Hinduism: the indifference of indestructible Being to those transitory acci-
dents which are birth and death; the sameness of creation
and destruction; the inanity of our feeble good and feeble

evil, as man defines them, in the face of that terrible life which surpasses all forms. This Krishna who is truly a torrent of delights is connected to the most ancient conceptions of him by virtue of his enormous and divine bounty. Even though he is incarnated, the god remains too tumultuous, too indifferent, for the *Gita-Govinda* to have any relationship whatsoever to the tremulous, self-assured dialogues other poets have had with divinity—such as that poignant Sufi chant which, in Persia in the same twelfth century, sweetly evokes the Sole Beloved. There, God is more the Lover than the Friend.

We must avoid that mistake committed in our time by so many archaeologists who venture onto the terrain of anthropology, which consists in causing a more ancient past to color a more recent one—those for whom the old, primitive thought serves only as an unconscious substratum.

The Krishna of Jayadeva is no more reducible than the Attis of Catullus or the Adonis of Greek elegiacs to the simple terms of some tribal myth of fertility. It is with our own feelings that it deals, and with our own delights. The scholar who reduces a myth or a sexual rite to nothing more than its utilitarian and tribal meaning (thus disinfecting it too, consciously or not, of a disturbing eroticism) simplifies as well, to an excessive degree, the world of prehistory: the primitive has feelings as much as we do. But we must beware just as much of the more ethereal mistake which consists in seeing in the ardent legend merely a spiritual symbol, nothing more than a hidden allegory. To reduce the role of sexual ravishment in the *Gita-Govinda* is to deny the special characteristics of this *Laya-Yoga*, which endeavors, precisely, to attain the Absolute by means of powerful sensual energies. The poet himself has clearly defined his plan: "Here are expressed in poetic form the various ways of love which lead to the quintessential comprehension of eroticism." Sensual pleasure in Jayadeva should not be treated as a kind of fleshly bait which is then discarded in favor of a meaning thought to be more noble; that is to risk leaving on our lips the taste of ambiguity or hypocrisy. Like the Lingam-Yoni before which those exquisite princesses of Moghul miniatures prostrate themselves, the sexual object is in itself both manifestation and symbol. The orgasm of Radha is indeed the ecstasy of the soul possessed by god, but that soul throbs within human flesh.

"The peacocks dance with joy . . . The cows run up, still chewing their cud, and the calves all frothy with the milk from their mothers. The animals shed soft tears at the sound of the Shepherd's flute . . ." says, more or less, the ancient *Bhagavata Purana*. Neither Jayadeva's work nor the carvings on temples give much place to the legend of this delicious presence of the animals, which, in contrast, fills the more tender pictures of Moghul miniatures, where Krishna, dressed as a milkmaid, milks the cows with his beloveds. And yet this presence of the animals plays a considerable role in the sacred idyll: divine ecstasy and human happiness cannot do without the calm contentment of the humble creatures who are exploited by man and who share with him in the adventure of living. It is, above all, in love that the Greeks joined their animals to their gods. One inadequately appreciates the unique beauty of the Hindu myth so long as one doesn't recognize, along with the most passionate sensuality (and perhaps precisely because this sensuality flows out almost without restraint), this candid friendship for beings of another species and other realms of being.* This tenderness, no doubt the result of the old animist thought but long since having transcended it to become a very aware form of the unity of all beings, remains one of the most beautiful of India's gifts to humanity: Christian Europe has scarcely known it, except in the Franciscan eclogue alone.

---

* Scenes of bestiality figure from time to time in Hindu bas-reliefs and erotic painting, but they don't appear to involve animal-gods. They have an almost childlike simplicity and gaiety.

Nowhere, perhaps, does the sacred legend find a more delicious expression than in a cult object from southern India, now in the Musée Guimet in Paris: a wood bas-relief on which Krishna is depicted dressed as a shepherd, playing his flute to the animals of the herd. Only his four arms evoke the all-powerful divine energy in this delicately human depiction: two hands hold the instrument; two hands are raised in benediction. This rather late work (some scholars place it as late as the seventeenth century) is one in which, beyond the Hinduist opulence of style, that distant Greek influence which marked Hindu art from its beginnings is best perceived. The curve of the Blue God's hips is almost Praxitelean; his long, undulating pantaloons differ very little from those given by Greco–Roman art to its youthful Asiatic gods, its Attises or its Mithrases. A silent melody, in which we recognize those poignant harmonies, both physiological and holy, of India, flows out from the lips of the god over the dense foliage, the animals, and the indolent, rhythmic forms of the divine posture. This lonely song helps us better understand the frenetic throbbings of the Gopis around the pillars of the temples, the great leaping movement of the thousand enraptured couples in the forest who themselves constitute the forest of beings. *Et Venus in silvis jungebat corpora amantium*, says Lucretius grandly. What India adds to this immense, cosmic pastoral is the profound sense of the one in many, the pulsation of a joy which courses through plant, animal, god, and man. Both blood and sap obey the sounds of the holy flutist; for him, the positions of love are the patterns of dance.

10

FESTIVALS
OF THE PASSING
YEAR

Commentary
on Christmas

The time of commercial Christmas is already here. For almost everyone—except for the poor, who constitute a large number of exceptions—it is a warm, bright interlude in the gray time of winter. For most of the celebrants today, the great Christian feast is limited to two rites: buying, more or less compulsively, useful or unuseful objects, and gorging themselves, or the people in their intimate circle, on an endless mélange of sentiments composed equally of the wish to give pleasure, ostentation, and the need to give oneself a good time. And let us not forget the evergreen pine trees cut from the forest, very ancient symbols of the everlasting vegetal world, which will die in central heating, nor the chair lifts that pour skiers out onto the virgin snow.

Being neither Catholic (except by birth and tradition) nor Protestant (except for some reading and the influence of certain great exemplars) nor even Christian, probably, in the full sense of the term, I am all the more drawn to celebrate this festival which is so rich in tradition and in its train of minor feasts—the northern Saint Nicholas and Saint Lucy, Candlemas and Twelfth Night. But let us stay with Christmas, the festival for everybody. It is concerned with a birth, and a birth such as births should always be, that of a child awaited with love and respect, carrying within himself the hope of the world. It is concerned with the poor: an old French ballad depicts Mary and Joseph meekly looking in Bethlehem for lodgings within their means, everywhere shown the door in favor of more illustrious, richer clients, and finally insulted by an innkeeper who "detests poverty." It is the festival of men of goodwill (as an ancient formula has it which, unhappily, one no longer always finds in modern versions of the Gospels), from that deaf-mute servant in medieval tales who assists Mary in her childbirth, to Joseph warming the newborn's swaddling clothes before a faint fire, even to the greasy shepherds deemed worthy of a visit from the Angel. It is the festival of a race too often despised and persecuted, since it is as a Jewish baby that the Newborn of the great Christian myth appears on earth (and, of course, I use the word *myth* with the greatest respect, as the ethnologists of our day use it, as signifying those great truths which are beyond us but which we need in order to live).

It is the festival of the animals who participate in the holy mystery of this night, a wonderful symbol whose importance Saint Francis and several other saints have recognized but which too many Christians of the current mold have neglected and neglect to take as an inspiration. It is the festival of the human community, since it is, or will be in a few days, the festival of the Three Kings, one of whom, according to legend, was black—an allegory of all the races on earth who bring their different gifts to the Child. It is a festival of joy, shaded with pathos, since this little baby who is worshipped will one day become the Man of Sorrows. Finally, it is the festival of Earth itself, whom one often sees depicted on Eastern icons prostrate at the threshold of the grotto where the Child chose to be born—of the Earth which, in its revolutions, passes at this moment the winter solstice and leads us all towards Spring. And that is why, long before the Church fixed this date for the birth of Christ, it was already, in antiquity, the Feast of the Sun. It seems to me appropriate to recall these things, which everyone knows but which so many of us forget.

1976

The Days of Easter:
One of the World's
Most Beautiful Stories

Leaving aside, at least for now, the ceremonies and rites of the holiest of the Christian weeks, I want to extract from the sacred texts which are read (but not always heard) in church those elements which would strike us if we found them in Dostoevsky or in Tolstoy or in some biography or other account of the life of a great man or a great victim. In short, the unfolding of one of the world's most beautiful stories.

An almost ironic prologue: some poor people arrive in the capital with their beloved master, who is acclaimed by that same populace which will soon boo him. A frugal holiday repast: a traitor discerned among the twelve guests; a simple soul who loudly proclaims his devotion and will be the first to falter; the youngest and the most beloved leaning almost indolently on his master's shoulder, enveloped as he probably is in that gilded cocoon which so often shields youth; the master, isolated by his wisdom and his prescience in the midst of these weak, ignorant souls who remain the best men he has found to follow him and continue his work.

Night having fallen, this master is even more alone in a bit of orchard high above the city, where everyone has forgot him except his enemies; the long, dark hours during which prescience turns into agony; the victim who prays that he may be spared the anticipated test, but who knows also that that cannot be and that, "if he had it to do over again," he would follow the same road; "the eternal soul" who keeps his vow "despite the lonely night." (Let Aragon and Rimbaud help us understand Mark and John.) While he suffers, his friends sleep, incapable of sensing the urgency of the moment. "What, could ye not watch with me one hour?" No: they couldn't; they were sleepy; and he who calls to them is not unaware that the time will come when these poor wretches will also have to suffer and keep a vigil.

The arrival of the multitude, ready to arrest the condemned man. The hotheaded defender, who risks making everything worse and is almost immediately deflated. The two establishments, ecclesiastical and secular, who pass the accused back and forth in their embarrassment; the eternal dialogue of fervor and skepticism vying with each other: "Everyone that is of the truth heareth my voice"—"What is truth?" The top civil servant, out of his depth, who would gladly wash his hands of the affair, leaving it up to the mob to choose which prisoner should be liberated in celebration of the approaching feast day; and the one chosen is, naturally, the famous criminal and not the innocent, just man. The condemned man abused, beaten, tortured by big brutes, many of whom are probably fine family men, good neighbors, nice guys; forced to drag his own gallows pole, just as, sometimes in prison camps, prisoners drag a shovel to dig their own grave. The small group of friends who stay with the man about to be executed, accepting the humiliation and danger that loyalty brings with it. The bickering of the guards arguing over the cast-off garments, just the way, in wartime, the comrades of a dead man sometimes fight over his cartridge belt or his shoes.

Tenderness dawning in the form of words of last advice to his followers, coming from one who until then had been too taken up with his mission to give much thought to them: the dying man giving his best friend to his mother as her son. (So, in our own time and in every land, the last letters of condemned men or of soldiers leaving on a mission from which they will not return are filled with advice about the marriage of their sisters or the pension of their aged mothers.) The words exchanged with a common criminal recognized as a man of heart; the long death in the sun and bitter wind, in full view of the mob, who bit by bit disperse, since it looks as though it will never end. That exclamation which seems to indicate that despair, too, is a state which must be endured if all is to be achieved: "Why hast thou forsaken me?" And, a few hours later, those poor people will manage to obtain the favor of a tomb for their dead one, and the sentries will sleep against the wall like (one must be careful of comparisons) those tired, humble companions earlier who had slept beside the living man in his agony.

What else? The hours, days, weeks which then unfold, somewhere between grief and confidence, between ghost and God, in that twilight atmosphere in which nothing is completely established, verified, conclusive, but through which passes the faint breeze of the inexplicable—as it does in some of those feeble reports made to societies for the advancement of psychic knowledge, so troubling because so inconclusive. The former prostitute come to the cemetery to weep and pray, believing she recognizes, in the guise of a gardener, the man she has lost. (What finer name for him who caused so many seeds to sprout in the human soul?) And later, when emotions have calmed down a bit (as it says in police reports), the two disciples walking down a road, joined by a friendly traveler who agrees to share a table with them at the inn and who disappears at the moment they realize it is He. One of the world's most beautiful stories ends with the reflections of a Presence, rather like those clouds that are still colored by the sun which has already sunk below the horizon.

"I'd feel closer to Jesus if he had been shot instead of crucified," a young officer who had fought in Korea once told me. It is for him and for all those who don't manage to uncover the essential beneath what might be called the accessories of the past that I've taken the risk of writing the above.

1977

Fires of the Solstice

The winter solstice has Christmas as its festival; Easter, at the spring equinox, occupies all by itself the place of other festivals of renewal, such as that May Day which the beauties and gallants of the Middle Ages celebrated by riding into the woods or dancing on meadows, or those Rogation Days which have become virtually outdated, as the men of today love neither earth nor heaven enough to invoke the blessings of the one upon the other. The Feast of Saint John, the festival of the summer solstice, has had its fires of joy extinguished almost everywhere, except perhaps in Scandinavian countries, where their tall flames are reflected upon the water of the lakes. But no one in Sicily any longer watches at dawn on June 24 to see Salomé dancing naked in the rising sun, bearing on a golden platter which is itself a solar image the head of the Baptist. There are exceptions; scattered here and there the old rites survive. In Greece and in Portugal, there is the ceremony of walking barefoot on burning embers, which is more ancient than Christianity itself. Florence has its fireworks, and in Greece and some small villages of France children roll in front of them wheels adorned with candles. But all this is hardly connected in people's minds with the antique glory of *sol invictus*.

And, indeed, this man of the desert nourished with honey and locusts, this prophet burned by the shimmering of the noonday sun on the rocks, this preacher with words of fire, can be a good symbol in the Middle East for the scorching season; the refreshing contrast of the river Jordan only increases its intensity. Yet it would appear that that element of splendor and luminous serenity, so closely associated in our temperate regions with the very idea of the June solstice, is sorely missing in this story of asceticism and blood. There are other Christian festivals of summer—Pentecost, with its mystical flames, and Corpus Christi, with its rustic, floral profusion around the monstrance; but they have never been felt to be *the* festivals of summer. That season which is a festival in itself lacks, properly speaking, a festival of its own.

Nevertheless, it would appear that in France our Chinese lanterns and fireworks on the Quatorze Juillet and in the United States the avalanche of firecrackers and Roman candles on the Yankee Fourth of July answer man's age-old need to reproduce on earth a great solar episode, to add a bit more, if he can, to the heat and light which fall from the sky. And one cannot regret too much that those ancient fires of joy which traveled from village to village and from summit to summit, threatening the forests and the high grass with conflagration, have been definitively extinguished, however picturesque the leaps of the dancers jumping around or over the flames must have been. Our dances in the streets and in the dance halls, themselves almost obsolete, have in their own way taken their place, but they are desacralized, except perhaps for a few drops of patriotism, instilled into the consciousness of the dancers by some of the *images d'Epinal* out of our history. And it may be that the vast, almost panicky summer exodus of today is some solar rite without a name.

Yet, at the very thought of a solstitial festival, a curious sort of vertigo overtakes us, like that of a man balancing on a slippery sphere. That full measure of light, that longest day of the year, which lasts almost ten weeks at the North Cape, is also the moment in Antarctica when night reigns, illumined only by the distant fires of the stars. What is more, this apogee signals the beginning of a descent; from now on, the days will get shorter and shorter, until they reach the nadir of the winter solstice; the astronomical winter begins in June, just as the astronomical summer begins in December, when the hours of light imperceptibly grow longer again until they reach the pinnacle of the Feast of Saint John. We have before us three months of green meadows, flowers, harvests, warm sand on the beaches, and songs in the branches; but the movement of the skies is already preparing our winter, as, in the depths of winter, it prepares the summer. We are caught in this rising and falling double helix. "Verweile doch, du bist so schön," Faust could have said to the June solstice. But he would have said it in vain. It is within ourselves, and without too much hope or belief, that durability must be sought.

1977

Days of the Dead

Any child born into a Catholic family of Western Europe has at least one memory of walking to the cemetery on the Day of the Dead, generally in cold, dull, gray weather. The day before was All Saints', a somewhat second-rate festival, not celebrated with gifts and food like Easter or Christmas, but a day which one knew was in honor of those dead who had been officially elevated to heaven. To be sure, there were thousands and thousands of saints. But there were as well—the child was already aware—thousands and thousands of dead whose fate in the next world was unknown, and the twenty-four hours of November 2 seemed much too short a time to pay tribute to all of them. They, too, were dead people who had risen to heaven, only without the ceremony of beatification and therefore without one's being completely sure about them; dead people temporarily in purgatory or definitively in hell; dead people from pagan times; dead people of other religions from other parts of the world, or even from here. In short, dead people—as dead as that dog or cow not seen again during your vacation who, you'd been bluntly told, had perished. For myself, I always link that lengthy visit to the cemetery with displays of chrysanthemums, those great globes that are always lavishly present on well-kept graves, since they are almost the only sprays offered by florists in that season, unless you want to do so much as a dozen roses, which wilt too quickly to make a very good show for very long.

There were, to be sure, some people in mourning who seemed truly sad. But what one mostly saw (and in this matter a child's eyes are pitiless) were well-dressed people, here approving and there criticizing the floral offerings left on graves other than their own by the owners of neighboring "concessions." And I shall never forget what I so often felt in cemeteries in France, the shock of horror at seeing flowers still pinned in their paper wrappings, which were like winding sheets in which they would end up rotting, with the tag of some good florist stuck on them—flowers which the givers, who loved neither the dead nor the flowers, had just dropped there without taking the trouble to bring a jar of water or even to strew them lovingly over the earth or the marble of the dead. It was enough to have bought these visiting-card bouquets (one must do one's duty) and to leave them there, possibly with a discreet Sign of the Cross if one remained faithful to the old customs, before getting away as fast as was decently possible, since the November weather did not encourage long vigils at the graveside.

What the rather bored, rather discouraged child didn't know was that these autumnal rites are among the oldest celebrated on earth. It appears that in every country the Day of the Dead occurs at the year's end, after the last harvests, when the barren earth is thought to give passage to the souls lying beneath it. From China to Northern Europe, the corpse placed in the earth, often covered with a grassy tumulus, served both to assure the fecundity of the fields and to protect them against enemy incursions, like the bones of old Oedipus in his tholos at Colonus. Always, the annual return of the dead, at this time when his ascent to the living is easiest, is as much feared as hoped for by

his descendants. Every rite is double-edged: with good conscience we make offerings destined to assure the survival of
the dead and at the same time to neutralize the noxiousness
he has acquired in becoming a dead man; but we take it for
granted that, once the festival of rediscovery is over, he will
be good enough to go back to his home in the earth. The
rites of the Day of the Dead are as much those of fear as
they are those of love. Once in Finland I was shown some
signposts and nameplates bearing the names of isolated
houses and farms which had been moved or shrouded with
opaque material so that the ghosts, disoriented, could not
come and install themselves again in their former lodgings.
It is an unadmitted and almost inadmissible fact that even
the most beloved dead, after several years or even several
months, would, were they to return, be intruders in the
existence of the living, whose circumstances have changed.
This is decreed not so much by men's egotism or fickleness
as by the exigencies of life itself.

There are exceptions to this rule of autumnal, funereal
commemorations. One of the most beautiful festivals of the
dead, the Bon festival, which is Buddhist, takes place in
summer and consists of launching on the sea hundreds of
tiny skiffs in which a little lamp is burning—the image of
our immense, precarious voyage to eternity. Less symbolic
perhaps, except insofar as they are emblems of the everlasting light we hope will shine over the dead, are the lanterns lighted on Christmas Eve in the cemeteries of
Scandinavia and Germany, as if one were lovingly inviting
those who exist no longer to share in the joy and thanks-
giving of the living. When one has once seen them on the
way to church in the lighted village, one can never forget
those little flames mirrored by the frozen ground or sparkling in the crystals of snow. Another exception to the rule
of autumnal festivals is the quasi-secular so-called Deco-
ration Day, which in the United States takes place towards
the end of May and consists in putting flowers on graves.

From a horticultural perspective alone, the time is well chosen: not only are there lots of flowers, but something of the amateur gardeners' enthusiasm for planting their gardens extends to the cemetery as well. In New England, a region of late springs, it often occasions the first picnic of the season. Without going so far as to eat and drink on the graves themselves, as is done in certain Islamic countries, nevertheless the living incorporate a thought for the dead in their enjoyment.

On the other hand, the real Day of the Dead in the United States is that burlesque and at times sinister masquerade of children and adolescents, Hallowe'en—the eve also of the first day of the month of Athyr in ancient Egypt, the anniversary of the death of Osiris, killed by the forces of Evil and become a sort of god of the dead. *Hallowed all*: all souls are sanctified. Except for a few scholars, no one is conscious of the original etymological sense of the word or connects this disorderly sabbath with a feast of the dead; and yet the true festivals, those most deeply rooted in the human unconscious, are those we celebrate without knowing why.

At Hallowe'en, it is not a matter of decorating cemeteries, or even of going there. It is a day of childish gaiety, for which mothers make simple and sometimes gloomy costumes for their darlings: there is hardly an American who does not recall the enchantment of having worn on that day a devil's fiery cap, the whiskers and tail of a cat, or a skeleton appliquéd in white on black cloth—a candid foretaste of metamorphoses. Dressed up like that, or as a witch, a ghost entangled in a bedsheet, Dracula, or Superman, and always with the appropriate masks, they go about from door to door begging candy, putting on a deep voice and threatening the inhabitants who don't give them treats or who give too few. Older children or adolescents go with them, or else form rival groups of their own, equally dressed up, costumed, wearing masks; and often there are lawless acts: broken or smeared windows, eggs thrown at windows or doors, garden furniture smashed, panes broken in an attempt at forced entry to get the coveted bottle of whiskey. Sometimes, too, appalling farces are perpetrated by adults who are annoyed by these intrusions: I have heard of slices of cake frosted with shaving cream or excrement or even, once, powdered with ground glass. It's also the night when girls scatter after a dance, risking more than ever being raped or even strangled behind a hedge.

On the roads, people put direction signs in the wrong place or turn them around, as the superstitious Finnish peasants do, for reasons best known to themselves. By another unconscious return to one of the world's oldest rites, a tree (always the same) in the center of the village where I live is covered with streamers by boys who climb it; they hang from every branch and wave in the wind, but, conveniently—because one has it at hand, or perhaps out of some scatological intention—masses of unrolled toilet paper replace the bits of cloth or rice paper of other civilizations. What once was fervor has turned into derision. In this great country which thinks of itself as materialist, these ghosts and carnival skeletons of autumn do not know what they are: spirits of the escaped dead that one is willing to feed in order then to chase them away with a combination of fun and fear. Rites and masks are more powerful than we.

1982

11

WHO KNOWS WHETHER THE SPIRIT OF ANIMALS GOES DOWNWARD

Who knoweth the spirit of
man that goeth upward, and
the spirit of the beast that
goeth downward to the earth?

ECCLESIASTES 3:21

Ο ne of the tales in *The Thousand and One Nights* recounts
that the earth and the animals trembled on the day when
God created man. This admirable poetic vision takes on
special significance for us, who know far better than the
medieval Arabian storyteller to what extent the earth and
the animals had reason to tremble. When I see cattle or
horses in a field—a splendid sight appreciated in all ages
by painters and poets as an "idyll" but now, alas, become
quite rare in our Western world—or even when I see a few
chickens still freely pecking away in a farmyard, I naturally
tell myself that these animals sacrificed to man's appetite
or worn out in his service will one day die a "bad death"
—bled to death, clubbed to death, strangled, or, following
the old custom when it's a question of a horse who isn't
being sent to the "horse butchers," killed with a bullet, often
badly aimed and almost never constituting a coup de grâce,
or abandoned in the wastes of the sierra as the peasants of
Madeira continue to do, or else (in what country is it I've
been told this is true?) prodded with a goad to a precipice
over which they fall and are broken.

Yet I tell myself that even at that moment, and probably
for months and years before, these animals have lived in

the open air, in full sunlight and full night, often badly treated, sometimes treated well, following more or less normally the cycles of their animal existence just as we are resigned to fulfilling the cycles of our own life. But this relative "normality" is no longer the norm today, when frightful overproduction (which in the end also degrades and kills man) turns animals into assembly-line products, passing their poor and brief existence (since the breeder has to recoup his money as quickly as possible) under the intolerable glare of electric lights, stuffed with hormones which transmit perils to us in their meat, laying their eggs and "doing their business" (as nurses and wet nurses used to say), deprived, if they are fowls confined in close quarters, of their beaks and claws, which, in their horrible packaged existence, they would otherwise turn against their fellow sufferers; or else, like the handsome steeds of the Garde Républicaine when they are old and broken, sent away to die, sometimes over a period lasting as long as two years, in a stall of the Institut Pasteur, where their sole diversion is to be bled every day, until finally, void of blood, they crumble, equine tatters which are the victims to our progress in immunology. The men of the Garde themselves exclaim that they would much rather see them sent straight to the butcher shop.

And almost all of us have, to be sure, used serums, even while hoping for a time when this particular medical advance will no longer be in vogue, as so many others have gone out of fashion. Most of us eat meat, although some abstain and dream with muted irony of the lessening of terror and suffering, of the consumed cells of a nutritive cycle which has ended in the jaws of those eaters of beefsteak.

Here, as elsewhere, equilibrium has been destroyed. The dreadful primal animal matter is a new thing, like those forests obliterated to furnish the pulp necessary for our daily and weekly papers filled with ads and false news, or like our oceans, in which the fish are sacrificed to the oil tankers. For thousands of years, men have thought of animals as belonging to them, yet a strict contract existed between them. The horseman loved his mount, even when he abused him. The hunter in earlier times knew the ways of game and, in his fashion, "loved" the animals he prided himself on killing—a kind of familiarity was mixed with the horror. The cow sent to the butcher when she had finally lost her milk and the pig bled to death for the feast of Christmas (the medieval wife of the swineherd traditionally sat on its trotters to prevent it from kicking) were, above all, the "poor beasts" for whom one cut grass and prepared meals of scraps. For more than one milkmaid, the cow against which she leaned to milk was a kind of mute friend. Caged rabbits lived only two steps away from the larder where they would end, "chopped into fine bits as meat for pâté"; but in the meantime they were the animals whose pink lips one loved to see twitching when you gave them some lettuce leaves through the wire of the cage.

We've changed all that: city children have never seen a cow or a sheep; and one doesn't love what one's never had a chance to get near or to caress. For a Parisian, the horse is scarcely more than that mythological beast, doped and pushed beyond his strength, on whom you can win some money if you bet right at the races. Cut into slices which are carefully wrapped in wax paper in the supermarket, or conserved in tins, the flesh of an animal ceases to be thought of as having once been alive. One finally comes to feel that our butchers' stalls, where animal quarters which have barely stopped bleeding hang from hooks (so atrocious a sight for anyone who isn't used to it that some of my foreign friends cross the street in Paris when they perceive it from a distance), are perhaps a good thing after all, inasmuch as they are visible testimonies of the violence done to animals by man.

At the same time, the fur coats displayed with such exquisite care in the windows of the big furriers' shops seem a million miles away from the seal who is bludgeoned to death with clubs on the ice floe or from the raccoon caught in a trap who tries to gnaw his own paw off in an effort to go free. The beauty who puts on makeup is unaware that her cosmetics have been tested on rabbits or guinea pigs who died sacrificed or blinded. The unawareness and, as a result, the clear conscience of the buyer is total, just as total as the innocence—the result of ignorance of what they're talking about, and a lack of imagination—of those who go to the trouble of defending gulags of different sorts or of approving the use of atomic weapons. A civilization that has moved farther and farther away from what is real creates more and more victims, including itself.

And yet the love of animals is as old as the human race. Thousands of written or spoken testimonials, of works of art and of witnessed acts, prove that. He loved his donkey, that Moroccan peasant who had just heard him condemned to death, because for weeks on end he had poured engine oil over his long ears covered with sores, since he thought it would be more effective because it was more expensive than the olive oil which was so plentiful on his little farm. Bit by bit, the horrible necrosis of the ears had rotted away the entire animal, who didn't have long to live but who would continue his labors until the end, since the man was too poor to allow him to be sacrificed. He loved his horse, that avaricious rich man who took the handsome gray animal for a free consultation with the European veterinarian; he had been the pride of the celebrations of Arab horsemanship, and it appeared that the only thing wrong with him was that he had been given poorly chosen feed. He loved his dog, that Portuguese peasant who every day carried in his arms his German shepherd with its broken leg, just to have him near during his long day's work in the garden, and to nourish him with the kitchen scraps. They love birds, that old man and old woman who feed the pigeons in shabby

Parisian parks and whom we do wrong to mock, since, thanks to the fluttering wings around them, they are entering into a rapport with the universe. He loved animals, the author of Ecclesiastes who asked if the spirit of beasts goes downward; or Leonardo, setting free the captive birds in the Florentine market; or that Chinese lady a thousand years ago who found a huge cage full of a hundred sparrows in a corner of her courtyard, which were there because her doctor had prescribed that she eat a still-warm brain every day. She flung wide the doors of the cage: "Who am I to take preference over so many little creatures?" Others before us have made the choices that continually confront us.

It appears that one of the chief causes of animal suffering, at least in the West, has been the biblical injunction from Jehovah to Adam before the Fall which showed him the world of animals, caused him to name them, and declared him their lord and master. This mythical scene has always been interpreted by the orthodox Christian and Jew as a permission to use as they want the thousands of species which express, by their forms different from ours, the infinite variety of life and, by their internal organization, their ability to act, to enjoy, and to suffer, the evident unity of life. And yet it would have been easy to interpret that ancient myth otherwise: that Adam still unsullied by the Fall might just as well have considered that he had been raised to the role of protector, arbitrator, and moderator of the whole of creation, using those gifts which had been given him beyond, or different from, those allotted to the animals in order to achieve and maintain the nice equilibrium of the world over which God had made him not the tyrant but the keeper.

Christianity might have emphasized those sublime legends which intermingle animal with man: the ox and the ass who warmed the Infant Jesus with their steamy breath; the lion who piously buried the bodies of the anchorites or who served as pet and guard dog for Saint Jerome; the crows who fed the Fathers of the desert and Saint Roch's dog who fed his master when he was ill; the wolf, the birds, and the fish of Saint Francis, the creatures of the woods who sought protection from Saint Blaise, the prayer for the animals of Saint Basil of Caesarea, or the stag with the crucifix in his antlers who converted Saint Hubert. (It is one of the cruelest ironies of religious folklore that this saint should subsequently have become the patron of hunters.) Or, also, the saints of Ireland and the Hebrides, who brought to shore and nursed wounded herons, who protected stags at bay, and who died in the company of a white horse. Christianity possessed all the elements of an animal folklore almost as rich as that of Buddhism, but it got carried away with arid dogmatism and the priority given to human egotism. It would appear that in this respect that movement which is supposed to be rationalist and secular and is called humanism (in the recent and abusive sense of the word) and which claims to be interested only in human applications is the direct heir of that impoverished Christianity from which knowledge and love of other beings has been stripped.

On the other hand, a different theory was to place itself at the service of those for whom the animal deserves no assistance and is deprived of the dignity which, at least in principle and on paper, we accord to each human being. In France, and in every country influenced by French culture, the animal-machine of Descartes has become an article of faith, all the easier to accept insofar as it favors exploitation and indifference. There, too, one may wonder if Descartes's assertion has not been received on the lowest possible level. The animal-machine, certainly—but neither more nor less a machine than man himself is a machine, a machine to produce and regulate the actions, impulses, and reactions which result from sensations of warmth and coldness, hunger and digestive satisfaction, sexual drive, and also grief, fatigue, and fear, which animals experience just as we do.

The animal is a machine; so is man. And it was no doubt the fear of blaspheming against the immortal soul which prevented Descartes from openly going further in this hypothesis, which would have laid the foundations of an authentic physiology and zoology. And Leonardo, had Descartes been able to know his *Notebooks*, would have whispered in his ear that at the furthest limit it is God Himself who is the "prime mover."

I've spoken rather at length of the animal drama and its primary causes. In the present state of the question, at a time when our abuses get worse in this matter as in so many others, one may wonder whether a Declaration of the Rights of Animals is going to be of any use. I greet it with joy; yet worthy people are already muttering: "It's almost two hundred years now since a Declaration of the Rights of Man was proclaimed, and what has been the result? No age has been more given to concentration camps, more tempted to massive destructions of human life, more ready, even among its very victims, to degrade the notion of humanity. Is there any point in promulgating on behalf of animals another document of this type, which, so long as man himself has not changed, will be as vain as the Declaration of the Rights of Man?" I believe there is. I believe it is always appropriate to promulgate or reaffirm the true Laws, even though they will continue no less to be broken, because it will leave transgressors here and there with the feeling of having done wrong. "Thou shalt not kill." All human history, of which we are so proud, is a perpetual infraction of that law.

"Thou shalt not cause animals to suffer, or, at the very least, thou shalt cause them to suffer as little as possible. They have their rights, as thou dost." That is surely a modest enough admonition; yet in the actual state of minds it is, alas, almost subversive. But *let* us be subversive. Let us revolt against ignorance, indifference, and cruelty, which in any case don't act quite so often against man only because they lay their hand on animals. Since we are compelled always to relate things to ourselves, let us remember that there would be fewer martyred children if there were fewer tortured animals, fewer sealed trains carrying the victims of whatever dictatorship to their deaths if we had not become accustomed to cattle cars in which animals die without food or water en route to the slaughterhouse, fewer human game felled with guns if the taste for and habit of killing were not the prerogative of hunters. And, within the humble measure of the possible, let us change—that is, let us improve if we can—life itself.

1981

12

THE SINISTER
EASE OF DYING

. . . And we must tremble so long as
we have not learned to heal
The sinister ease of dying.

I say to myself these verses of Victor Hugo, written almost a century ago about the dead of the Commune, whenever I think of those young men and that young girl who threw themselves into the flames rather than accept the world which had been made for them. Perhaps it is the first time in our Occidental society that a voluntary immolation like that has outraged the morality of vested interests, good sense, and the notion of adapting to the world as it is. But is such an immolation really voluntary? Like the Christians who once refused to sacrifice to idols, these young people felt, rightly or wrongly, that they had only the choice of sacrificing to the false gods of avidity and violence among which we agree to live or else of protesting with their deaths.

In one respect at least, they were not wrong: one cannot live without being implicated. "The world is on fire," the Buddhist sutras have said for almost three thousand years; "the fire of ignorance, the fire of lust, the fire of aggression is devouring it." Several young people in Lille, in Paris, and, only a few months ago, in Provence have recognized this truth which most of us spend our lives avoiding. They quit a world in which wars more radically destructive than ever take place amidst a peace which isn't really peace and tends too often to become as destructive as war itself for man and his environment, a world in which advertisements for gastronomic restaurants stand side by side in the newspapers with accounts of people dead from hunger, where every woman who wears a fur coat contributes to the extinction of a living species, where our passion for speed aggravates every day the pollution of a world on which we depend for life, where every avid reader of murder mysteries or of sinister news items and every spectator at films of violence contributes without knowing it to this passion for killing which has resulted in the millions of people put to death in the past half century. Were those young people right or wrong to leave all that?

The answer will finally depend on whether or not their sacrifice caused a change of heart in those around them. Could we have prevented them from taking this course of action? Or, more important, can we in the future prevent other pure hearts from following the same road? Confronted with this pressing question, we must admit that none of the usual reasons we might have given them for continuing to live is sufficiently compelling to restrain someone who can no longer tolerate the world as it is. It would be vain to tell them that the cleverest, or possibly the wisest, can still make their way through the chaos in which we find ourselves, or can even derive some bits of happiness or personal success from it, when what they die for is not their own distress but that of others.

It seems that against this Buddhist-monk type of sacrifice, so deserving of admiration in the very depths of its horror, one can usefully counterpose only the tradition which claims that Buddha himself, on the point of entering into peace, decided to remain in this world so long as one living creature needed his help. Those who have departed were surely of the best: we have need of them. Perhaps we might have saved them if we had persuaded them that their refusal, their indignation, their very despair were necessary; if we had known how to urge against the sinister ease of dying the heroic difficulty of living—or of trying to live—in such a way as to make the world a little less scandalous than it is.

1970

13

ANDALUSIA, OR THE HESPERIDES

Southern Spain has had many names: Baetica in Roman times, the Caliphate of Cordova, the Kingdom of Granada, and that old appellation from the time of the barbarian invasions, Andalusia—that is, the land of the Vandals. The oldest of its names remains the most meaningful: the Hesperides, the land of the setting sun.

There are two gates to the Mediterranean, the Hellespont in the east, and in the west the Pillars of Hercules (I omit the Suez, because that is a fissure made by the hand of man). One's knowledge of it is incomplete unless one takes into account these two straits and the regions they open or close. At the farthest edge of Spain, as on the borders of Asia Minor, Europe affirms itself at the same time that it completes itself. That East and that West have, for twenty centuries, oscillated like the two ends of a seesaw, whose fulcrum is Rome. As in the Greek archipelago, empires are won or lost here as the result of sudden squalls and the risks of combat at close quarters: Spain has Trafalgar, in the way the Levant has Actium or Lepanto. At Granada as at Constantinople, we find the farthermost point of the world of tent and desert placed within the bosom of the gardens of Europe. Cádiz, Ultima Gades, served as the gateway to the

Atlantic for the Greco–Roman world, in the same way that ancient Byzantium was the gateway to the Black Sea and to Asia. And the dry, light air of Seville, with its rhythm of life which is at once continental and maritime, inevitably reminds one of Athens.

Since prehistoric times, Spain has been approached from its left flank or at its point: what matters most in Andalusia was brought there in the hollow of Cretan, Greek, or Punic vessels, on the triremes of Rome, and on Moslem feluccas. However far back one goes into the past, it is impossible to reach a moment when the East, its African intermediaries, and Rome had not already left their mark on this lovely land. But Spain, and especially Andalusia, also resembles the Levant inasmuch as, Mediterranean though it is, it is only partly so. It overhangs the Atlantic the way Greece overhangs Asia. Its peripheral position as the western frontier of the known world slowed its entrance onto the universal stage: the colonial expansion of Greece and its unique and eternally youthful contribution to human experience are located in the beginnings of our history; Spain is very ancient, yet it developed later, ripened only in certain respects and withered prematurely in others, and achieved its destiny only in the fullness of the Renaissance. The abyss which borders its right flank was certainly less menacing than the great Asiatic mass which lies beyond Greece, since it was not invaded at regular intervals, the way Asia was by the hordes of Darius or of Timur. But that abyss was darker, more immeasurable, and more empty, related to the void and closer to the mysterious, inaccessible Atlantides.

From ancient times, the Greeks had vaguely situated somewhere beyond the Iberian coast their Island of Heroes, the Elysian Fields of Achilles, which another tradition places at the opposite end of the then known world, in the Black Sea. At the height of the Middle Ages, Dante, taking up this great Atlantic theme, led his Ulysses far from Ithaca to have him drown in sight of the Canary (or possibly the Cape Verde) Islands, under a sky in which different stars already shone and in latitudes the conquistadors would later know. But it is especially from the beginning of the sixteenth century, near the time when through heraldic chance the image of the Golden Fleece began to haunt the courtiers of Charles V, that the Atlantic effectively became the Ocean Sea, whose Argonauts were Columbus, Pizarro, and Cortés and whose Colchises were Florida and Mexico. The barrenness and strength of that land and the vast uninhabited spaces of its plateaus and sierras link Spain, as it were, with those lands beyond the Ocean almost devoid of history. The port of Sanlúcar de Barrameda, from which the first galleons steered their course westward; the monastery of La Rábida, where Columbus dreamed of his voyage, and the Archives of Seville, where the charts and mappemondes of the great explorers are piously preserved are the places where a planetary image of the world imposed itself on man.

The little provincial museum of Cádiz contains a Punic sarcophagus, brother to the Sidonian sarcophagi in the Louvre: a heavy anthropoid form, its arms bent in one of those poses habitual to the dead, its hand holding a pomegranate or a heart. The inside of the sarcophagus reveals a skeleton as vigorous as the trunk of a tree. This unknown Punic man sums up in advance one of the great experiences of Spain: the Arabs will follow the Carthaginians; Catholic Spain of the Reconquista will, in its fashion, take up again the task of the Spain of the Scipios; Saguntum and Numantia, faithful unto death and the executioner's flames, the one to Rome, the other to Carthage, set up two contradictory examples of loyalty on Iberian soil. In Granada, the severe palace of Charles V stands in contrast to the Alhambra, through which blow the winds of the Islamic East. That mosque turned into a chapel in which the Catholic Queen wished to be laid to rest facing the conquered city signifies a moment of eternal Punic War. Beyond the

Carthaginian period, even older influences appear: in the bull rings of Seville one thinks of the tauromachies depicted on Cretan frescoes and of those hazardous acrobatics of the athlete which are observed from above by indolent female spectators. The Madonna of Good Friday, the Macarena glittering with jewels, has a sister in the dawn of time, the Lady of Elche in her Phoenician ornaments. A Greek art of modeling, or one inherited from the Greeks, contributed in one way or another to the articulation of these two pure idols; the hard, sensitive features are those of Iberian beauty, but the ardor, the steady gaze, and the heavy jewels come from the East.

Roman Spain lasted almost seven centuries, which constitutes by far the longest period of peace the peninsula has ever known. Everywhere on the map and soil of present-day Andalusia there blossom the towns, roads, aqueducts, ports, and monuments of that tranquil, overpopulated, prosperous Spain which supplied Rome with its leather, its salt meat, its esparto grass, and the ingots of its mines. Mosques and cathedrals rise on ancient ruins; the bridge of Cordova once bore the legions of Galba. Ronda encircled with mountains retains traces of Pompey; the memory of that great partisan, which spreads through all Spanish poetry, is still found today on walls covered with schoolboy graffiti. Italica, the birthplace of Trajan, Hadrian, and Theodosius, is more than three-quarters buried, but its mosaics and its few statues attest to a splendor which is the result of the efforts of Hellenized local artisans or else of the luxury of importations from Greece and Rome. For the noble Spanish poet of the seventeenth century, Rodrigo Caro, Italica remains the symbol of melancholy solitude, a dry riverbed left by the vast flood of a life that is gone. The people of Seville are fond of quoting that phrase of Hume which states that the two Andalusian emperors who succeeded each other in Rome made possible one of the rare beautiful centuries humanity has known: Seville has its Trajan Street and its Hadrian Street.

Historians have endeavored to define the nature of this infiltration of Rome by the Spanish clan, a phenomenon which recurred again much later, in the time of the Borgias: some have attempted to find eternal Ibernian characteristics in Hadrian, here in his taste for colossal constructions, there in his taste for funeral pomp. Some have thought they saw a latent Hispanism in the excesses of a Seneca or a Lucan, or in the aesthetic nihilism of Marcus Aurelius. One can just as easily reverse the terms of the problem and ask if those wrinkles so strongly marked with Spanish temperament or thought were not furrowed by the lasting influence of Rome. Let us not forget that this Stoic individualism, this baroque passion, and this imperial taste for universal domination will not reappear on the peninsula until more than a thousand years after the fall of Rome, reintroduced then by Renaissance Italy. In the end, it appears that Spain did not inherit anything directly from its Roman ancestry except that oldest part of its patrimony which is least touched by ideologies and cultures and most shared by the entire Mediterranean region and its bundle of races; yet in Spain that part remained more unalterable and evident than elsewhere: the dance which is reminiscent of the swaying and twisting of the girls of Gades, the delight of debauched Romans; the cooking with its fried, salted, and raw foods and the predominance of lentils and beans just as in a menu out of Martial or Horace; the circus with its bloody sport; the profound *religio* that imbues its sacred places and holy statues; the austere, patriarchal sense of family which tempers the strong appetite for pleasure and bodily freedom; and, more important than all that, the very disposition of the house itself, its atrium, patio, and courtyard with babbling fountain.

After the Roman peace came Arab prosperity: that, too, lasted almost seven centuries. The Arab tide ebbed only slowly from Spain, at the very moment when, by some curious phenomenon of balance, the Turkish tide came flooding in over the Christian East: the loss of Granada follows by only forty years the conquest of Constantinople. That is merely to say that Islam in Spain has the advantage over its counterpart in the Greek East of being closer to the sources, the origins, and the Hegira. The palace of Medina Azzahra near Cordova is nothing more than a heap of pulverized debris, yet it remains impressive: it is an Asia far older than Islam; it is a potential Achaemenid Persia. It's the melancholy verses of Persian poets on those royal palaces which will henceforth be haunted by wild asses and gazelles that one thinks of in those empty rooms and in the presence of that bronze stag in whom a centuries-old technique is manifested, of those stuccos and shards on which an obsession with animal forms is dissembled in arabesques and foliated scrolls. Despite the brief hiatus of the Vandals and Visigoths, what is Arabian in Spain is generally superimposed directly upon the antique: the art of a civilization for whom every delight and geometry ended in the human form saw itself replaced by an art dedicated only to the modulation of lines which stretch out, interlace, embrace, and signify nothing but themselves, an abstract music, an eternal mathematical meditation. In Cordova, threshold of a culture fed by Moslem fervor, Jewish subtlety, and certain Hellenic concepts passed through the alembic of Arab thought, the throng of alchemists, algebrists, and astronomers achieved in the Mosque the most complete of transformations, the most complex equations, the perfect equivalent of the secret cogitations of Averroës or Avicenna. These mute harmonies are those of the spheres.

The Arabian art of Granada, later and more feminine, is addressed to the spirit through the senses. Such a linear suavity cancels out all historical pictorialness: the throat-cutting of the Abencerrages or the flight of Boabdil are as nothing amidst those stucco prisms and stars, under those vaults which seem to have stolen from corollas, grottoes, and honeycombs their profoundly natural secret which is yet so distant from the human. This almost vegetal perfection goes beyond unity of style, does not depend on authenticity of detail, and endures all injury with an enchanting docility: the Generalife, with its eroded surfaces, its rebuilt pavilions, and its groves retouched by modern gardeners, remains what its Arab builder hoped it would be: a paradise of agreeable meditations and easy pleasures. At the thought of other destroyed or ruined Granada palaces, one doesn't feel the bitter chagrin that overcomes us when we see the wounds of the Parthenon or are on the site of a bombed cathedral: one accepts that these beautiful objects have flourished and faded like narcissi.

The gothic art of Andalusia is a military art, planted there by the Reconquista, brought from the North like a sort of armed monk. Although it became indigenous, it early bore the imprint of Mudejar hands. More liberal than the religion or the local customs, it accepts mixed marriages and secret adulteries. The Cathedral of Seville, that enormous fortress of Catholic faith, hangs its bells in the Moslem Giralda and keeps utterly hidden from itself its Arab courtyard of orange trees. But Sevillian gothic is merely the exception that proves the rule: almost everywhere, it is the art of the Renaissance (regularly qualified as Greco Roman in Spanish handbooks) and its baroque developments which proclaim the definitive victory of the West in Andalusia. Even in Cordova, although it was reconquered from Islam more than two centuries before Granada and twenty years before Seville, the evisceration of the cathedral dates only from the time of Charles V: the baroque was given the charge of attesting to, if not the truths of faith, at least the vainglory of the canons. This art which is all pomp and circumstance assails the visitor from the moment when, from arch to arch, from colonnade to colonnade, he draws near to the center of the edifice, and it shatters, as if with a bomb, one of the most noble meditations ever performed on plenitude and emptiness, on the structure of the universe, and on the mystery of God. It is within Renaissance and baroque décors that the trials of the Inquisition took place down to the eighteenth century. It is in a Renaissance chapel that Isabella the Catholic reposes after her crusading frenzies. But this Renaissance and baroque are not, as in Italy, the affirmation of a new, secular will to live or the cry of pride of some pope or prince. The palace of Charles V at Granada, considered by itself and not in relation to the Alhambra, which it overwhelms, is one of the most handsome examples of Renaissance architecture, yet its severity and harshness far exceed that of the Roman or even the Florentine palaces which inspired it. Its plan may well have been taken from the Roman villa of Julius II; it no more resembles it than a man in armor resembles a man dressed in silks. A thought which remained medieval fills these Italianate churches, where in other countries we are accustomed to look for nothing more than a completely human religious rhetoric; the emptiness of terrestrial glory manifests itself here through antiphrasis, as, for example, in that sacred, empty burial vault in Granada, that charnel house of sorts, where four decaying sarcophagi are lined up beside each other under the pompous tombs of the Catholic Kings.

The interiors of the chapels of Seville are pervaded with the same black-and-gold intimacy as a Byzantine oratory, from which they are in any case directly descended in this land where Vandal Arianism preceded Islam. What is more, the infinite repetition of detail, the proliferation of forms, and the obsessive multiplicity of divine and human figurations often remind one more of Hindu temples than of Roman basilicas. The baroque, that violent art intended to impress the masses, here represents not merely a taciturn race's achievement of grandiloquence; it becomes the normal mode of expression for a people henceforth accustomed to extreme tensions, weaned from the serene abstractions of Arab and Mudejar art, and for whom the poise of Greco–Roman art has become fundamentally alien. The most baroque manifestations of Andalusian art are also those most rooted in the Christian Middle Ages or in an ancient, non-Christian past even farther back: the pomp of tauromachic processions; the embroidered costumes of the toreros, often ripped and bloody, which are then mended by tiny hands in some dressmaker's establishment in Seville; the costumes of the Corpus Christi dancers, as crimson as the Nazarene who was whipped and displayed to the people, floating like a wave of blood over the heads of the crowd; the silverwork and catafalques of Good Friday.

The painting of Seville (and we may put under this rubric those painters born in Seville, like Murillo and Valdés Leal, those who did their apprenticeship there, like Velásquez, and those who made their careers there, like Zurbarán) is wholly contained within one century, the eighteenth, but its fruit is truly that of the Hesperides. These painters who were lifted to the skies by their individual lyricism or their pitiless realism are nonetheless strongly Italianate: there is nothing in their work which had not already occurred in the Venetians and in Caravaggio—nothing except, naturally, the temperament and the inimitable accent. Their favorite subjects are characteristically Spanish insofar as they testify to the choice of the artist or his Spanish patron in the seventeenth century; nevertheless, they follow the main currents of European Counter-Reformation art—religious melodramas, portraits of aristocratic clients or men of the Church, and genre scenes or still lifes inspired by the art of the North. Yet, in Spanish religious painting, a fervor inherited from the Middle Ages still sustains those forms of male and female saints who are otherwise so pompously oratorical or voluptuously soft. In portraits, the Spanish painter individualizes where the Italian painter personalizes: a great sixteenth-century Italian portrait is a meditation on beauty, ambition, or the flight of youth, or even on old age and guile, as in Titian's *Paul III*; however unique, these beings express more than themselves; they contain within themselves the highest aspirations or most hidden vices of the race; they are fleeting moments of an eternal theme. Here, in contrast, the profound Christianity and dark realism of Spain come together to clothe with tragic dignity and singularity that hunchback, that anemic Infanta, that vermin-ridden pauper, or that Knight of Calatrava, each marked with the individual characteristics he will carry to the grave, enclosed within a body through which he must seek damnation or salvation. Even in the greatest—Velásquez, for example, whose genius seems to draw classical conclusions from this perpetual confrontation of the moment with the object, lessons which we feel are universal—the meaning of those lessons remains a mystery to us for lack of evidence, just as the inner secrets and raison d'être of each individual we meet in life remain a mystery to us. No art is more stripped of metaphysics than this art which is so nourished with religious intentions: it is not death which is presented to us in that picture of Valdés Leal which Murillo claimed reeked with stench; it is a cadaver, and the cadaver is a portrait. Murillo's Saint Elizabeth is not a symbol of charity: she is a woman washing a man suffering from scurvy. In Zurbarán's or Alonso Cano's pictures of saints in ecstasy, we are not shown the beatific vision; we are shown the look of the visionary. This obsession with the individual marks the final victory of West over East, yet at the same time baroque showiness eliminates the last traces of Arab or Mudejar refinement. Moreover, whole areas of classical humanism will continue to remain foreign to Spanish painting—for example, the glory of the nude. The *Venus* of Velásquez is a masterpiece that goes against the current in this land dominated by Christian preconceptions and, more clandestinely, by Oriental atavism, and also, perhaps, too obsessed with detail, the accidental, and the momentary to take pleasure in the pure melody of form. In contrast, the *Maja desnuda* of Goya, which is not at all Andalusian and would not have shocked a Sevillian cigar-maker, enters the tradition of realism with its sensuous but ill-formed body. Even the swarthy, golden flesh of Murillo's little beggars is inseparable from their rags, which seem a part of their very being.

In genre scenes or still lifes, the Andalusian school asserts itself with this same typically Spanish *realism*—and to give that word its full force one must perhaps include the dialectical meaning it had in medieval philosophy. Not the Essence or the Idea, but the Thing Itself. Not the dreamy meditation of a Rembrandt or a Soutine on the secrets of matter, not the almost mystical vision of a Vermeer or the formal, intellectual rearrangements of a Chardin or a Cézanne. But the object itself—that fish, that onion, that pink, that lemon beside that orange. And perhaps it has not been sufficiently observed that these powerful realist painters of the School of Seville present only one point of view, extraordinarily intense, to be sure, but limited to certain almost obsessive aspects of Spain: the carefree languor of Seville is virtually absent. Until Goya, who will sketch the beautiful strollers of Madrid (and the ugly ones, too) or the hubbub of pilgrimages with the same clean line with which he elsewhere notes down an accident or a scuffle in some public square, Spanish painting had rarely attempted to render freely life out-of-doors and in full daylight. Flemish, Florentine, and Venetian painters, respectively, teach us far more about their sky and the air in their streets than the Sevillian painters of the Golden Age teach us about Seville.

.   .   .

Some countries die or cease young: everything that follows their brief period of vigor falls into the category of survival or resurrection. Spain never recovered from the fatigue of its imperial enterprises, from the easy gold of the New World, and from the bloodletting she inflicted upon herself in purging from her veins the last drops of Jewish and Moorish blood. Andalusia in particular suffered from this sort of auto-da-fé perpetrated to honor the Castilian ideal of the race. The Spanish legend and ideology are, properly speaking, Castilian: Andalusia melts away in the ardent chorus of Christian Spain, to which it adds only a few moving mystical or fleshly variations. Almost all of them take a quest as their theme: those historical and legendary figures all define themselves with that mighty word *quiero*, which means both "I love" and "I seek." Juana la loca following a coffin along the roads, brooding over her dead one; Juan de la Cruz looking out his window at the sublime spectacle of the Sierra Nevada and the Vega de Granada, thrusting from his mind those shapes only half discernible in the starlight, seeking God in the night; Miguel de Mañara going from woman to woman in the streets of the Barrio de la Cruz before ending his life dressed as a servant to the poor, having no doubt forgotten the sad voice of Elvira; and nearer to us, the insatiable Doña Belize and the pitiless Bernarda. Beautiful images, more or less isolated in the experience of the race, which show us above all what a people thought it found in itself that was essential. Land of poets which, again only yesterday, García Lorca watered with his blood. Land of poets especially in that it has been perpetually loved and re-created from a distance, in the complaints of Arab poets weeping over lost Granada and also in the work of Western poets from the other side of the mountains and the sea. For Miguel de Mañara to become and remain Don Juan, for the amorous quest of the Andalusian knight to serve as a pendant to the heroic and Castilian quest of Don Quixote in the history of human aspiration for the impossible, there had to be Tirso de Molina, there had to be, above all, Molière, and Mozart, and Byron, and that story of Balzac's, and those lines of Baudelaire, and, again in our day, that tragic farce of Montherlant.

Thus, we finally begin to understand what touches and sometimes unsettles us about this country: the direct contact with reality, the raw weight of the object, the emotion or feeling, strong and simple, old and ever new, hard as the rind or soft as the pulp of a fruit. This celebrated land is wonderfully unsoiled with literary artifice; even the preciosity of some of its poets does not affect it. This earth out of which so many masterpieces have sprung is not immediately felt to be, like Italy, one of the privileged fatherlands of the arts; yet life throbs in it like blood in the arteries. Few countries have been more devastated by the fury of wars of religion, race, and class; but if we tolerate the memory of so much inexpiable fury, it is because here it appears more naked, more spontaneous, and less hypocritical than elsewhere, almost innocent in its confession of the pleasure man takes in doing evil to man. No country is more dominated by a powerful religion which generally favors bigotry and intolerance; yet there is no country, either, in which one so senses human fervor welling up under the brocade of devotions or the rock of dogma. No country is more tied to, yet at the same time more free from, that rudimentary and supreme freedom which comes from stripping things down to their essence, from poverty, indifference, the joy of life, and scorn of death. Let us list its delights for us: Granada was beautiful, but that nightingale who sang every night, its dark throat swollen with song, taught us as much about Arab poetry as the inscriptions in the Alhambra. Beside the ocean at Cádiz, among buried stones which may be those of the temple of Hercules of Gades, that young boy with his brown legs, standing up to his thighs in water which was as pale blue as his washed-out rags, concentrating only on the rewards and disappointments of his fishing, moved us as much as the ancient statue we found at the water's edge. That aged, half-blind nun who showed us the paintings in the Hospital de la Caridad without seeing them herself takes her place in our memory beside the painted figures. The massive hugeness of the Cathedral of Seville seemed to be explained, or possibly justified, by the presence of a solitary woman praying with her arms raised. Somewhat less, or somewhat more, I think of those two peasants lying beside the road in their garments of striped wool, of that pile of sheep with their throats cut in a wagon at the door of a butcher shop, filled with the obscene, frank presence of death, of those somewhat limp flowers crushed in the warm hands of a beggar child, of the bread on that table insidiously encircled by a fly, of the pink juice spurting out of that pomegranate . . .

1952

14

OPPIAN, OR
THE CHASE

The *Cynegetica* ("The Chase") of Oppian belongs to that now dead genre of didactic works in verse which was esteemed all through antiquity. Even what little is known of its author is uncertain. It appears that the real Oppian, a Greek from Cilicia, limited himself to writing at about the time of Commodus a poem on fishing which was continued on the subject of hunting by another Greek poet, who was born in Apamea on the Orontes and was a contemporary of Caracalla. But for Florent Chrestien, who translated the *Cynegetica* around the middle of the sixteenth century, for all the Renaissance humanists, and above all for Buffon himself, who did not hesitate to imitate a passage from the *Cynegetica* in his celebrated description of the horse, the two poets were one. At all events, for a long time the *Cynegetica* especially continued to be very well known.

Didactic poetry remained in vogue throughout the Middle Ages and into the Renaissance, and occasionally even into the eighteenth century, not only for the pleasure of embellishing a subject with all the resources of poetic literature while at the same time making use of the riches of its own specialized vocabulary, but also as a serious method of teaching, perhaps even as a mnemotechnic device, as

poetry always more or less is anyway. Men of letters and
lovers of the Byzantine hunt continued to derive pleasure
and profit from this *Cynegetica*, which has come down to us
through some twenty manuscripts scattered in various European libraries. Henri II of France, a great huntsman,
valued Oppian so much that he had a manuscript copy made
for his own personal use; and that was probably one of the
last times, in that age when printing was already triumph-
ing, when a quill pen and parchment were put into service
for a Greek poet. One can imagine that the pages of that
royal Oppian were turned, somewhat distractedly, by the
beautiful hands of the Duchess of Valentinois, the huntress
Diana of the sixteenth century.

Born out of the need for a meat diet and the necessity of
defending oneself against wild animals, hunting became an
art, the most ancient of all, and a passion as well. Man
found that it satisfied his liking for risks and physical feats,
his vanity and boastfulness, and above all his innate ferocity.
Once he became a citizen, he saw in it a chance to reenter
periodically the barbarian world he basically never ceased
to miss. He embellished that violent sport with the learned
pleasures of dressage; he brought to it horses, dogs, and
sometimes birds of prey. He created a school of stratagem
out of it, a test of endurance, and often an occasion for
ostentatious display. And he never ceased to include in it
the sentiment of the sacred. The hunting horns in the Mass
of Saint Hubert (a saint whose legend ought to have given
all Christians a disgust for hunting) continue a tradition that
goes back to those paintings of animals depicted for magical
purposes by the magicians of prehistory and to tribal prayers uttered on the eve of hunting expeditions.

Ancient art and poetry made extensive use of this world
of movement and shouts, of furs and pelts, of nets set and
spears brandished, of shaken boughs, heroic nudity, and
floating draperies. The hunts and fishing expeditions on
Etruscan tombs, in which the artist has rendered the feeling

of swarthy bodies moving through the air and water of a
morning twenty-five centuries ago with an impressionism
avant la lettre; the hunts of Meleager nobly depicted on the
sides of Greek sarcophagi; the struggle of Hercules and the
lion contained within the orb of Italiot coins; the statues
of Diana dashing through thickets with her hind at her side.
Euripides gives us a romantic image of the hunts of Hip-
polytus, in which the scents of the woods and flowers gathered in the forest hide the stench and blood of the wild
beasts; Aristophanes speaks of the modest hunting parties
of common people on the outskirts of Athens; Virgil is no
doubt thinking of the sumptuous diversions of the patricians
of his day when he presents us Dido offering Aeneas a stag
hunt during which the amorous queen takes refuge in a cave
with the handsome stranger. But for the Classical Age these
representations of the oldest of sports represent above all a
return to the heroic times of legend or a simple glance at
the realities of the life of the common people: in Greece
they preferred to concentrate on the palaestra, where man
had only man for his companion and adversary; in Rome,
the important figures are above all presented in the exercise
of their public functions. We are not shown Pericles killing
partridges or Augustus chasing deer.

By the time of Oppian, everything had changed. That
nostalgia for the woods which overcame the citizen in the
broiling streets of Rome or Antioch, the romanticism of the
age, its materialism even more—all that contributed to placing this gaudy, savage sport in the foreground once more.
Those huge spectacles in the Circus, where thousands of
animals perished during staged hunts, gave the plebian the
equivalent of those pleasures which high functionaries and
great landowners like Oppian himself demanded from their
lands in Asia or Africa, in Gaul or Spain. A century earlier,
sculptors had already represented Hadrian galloping along-
side his favorite, Antinous, in quest of bear and boar; they
also depicted the two men with their feet on the lion of

Libya which they had just slain. Later, Commodus had gone lion hunting in public in the arenas of Rome. Caracalla himself, who grew up on the frontier, had introduced himself to these dangerous sports in the company of barbarian huntsmen. One hundred years later, a centurion stationed at Trier, on the edge of the great German forest, boasted of having killed fifty bears in six months. In a significant change, it is no longer man but the wild beasts who henceforth captivate the human imagination. They are everywhere in the mosaics of the period, covering the floors of Greco–Roman houses with their leaps and bounds. The work of Oppian presents an amazing catalogue of savage animals, from the lion to the onager and gazelle, from the elephant to the bear, from the tiger to the rhinoceros and crocodile. A wind that is already barbarian blows through this end of empire. It appears that this civilization, which was exhausting its resources, saw the tops of the forests, the sand dunes, the copses, and the moors, which they had for so long endeavored to conquer or to forget, grow bigger and draw closer to them.

In the sixteenth century, Florent Chrestien, keeper of the royal libraries and a good humanist who taught Henri IV, translated the *Four Books of Venery of Oppian*. This scholar also collaborated on the *Satire Menipée*, which indicates that he had his part in the bitternesses and outrages of his day. His choice of Oppian partly reflects the tastes of his powerful protectors: the book is dedicated to Henri de Navarre, who loved hunting. Every translator who is more than a mere laborer transposes, even without meaning to: for the noble Greek hexameters, like beautiful stallions with flowing manes, Florent Chrestien substitutes his alexandrines with their rather panting rhythm, racing one after the other, yoked together by rhyme, like hounds let loose two by two in the grass. While Oppian learnedly utilized the riches of a language and literature already grown old, Chrestian plays with the resources of a language at the moment of its rawest youth: his translation is a picturesque glossary of old French venery. Moreover, despite himself, Florent has a thousand years of uninterrupted medieval hunting behind him—that world, at once enticing and forbidding, of the haunted forest of werewolves and fairy hinds, filled with animals run to ground by serfs and pursued by the retinues of our kings. He had never seen the great wild beasts of Africa and Asia which were so familiar to the contemporaries of Oppian; at most he might have looked at the scrawny, caged lions in the moats of the Louvre. Thus, he cannot avoid giving to those creatures, which for him were half fabulous, the fantastic splendor of a coat of arms or a bestiary. At the same time, his stags, their does, and their décor of greenery have all the charm of a hunt depicted in a miniature or on a tapestry. Just as in the story of the magic hunt of Beau Pécopin, pursued across the centuries, hunters out of the time of Caracalla come into the Forest of Fontainebleau.

We must admire the superimposed layers of thought, experience, and labor out of which those old books which have come down to us are composed. A Greek poet who lived in Asia around the 245th Olympiad was edited in Paris in 1555 by a Renaissance scholar. The ancient roll of parchment, wrapped in red silk and rolled on a rod of ivory, became, through the intermediary of medieval manuscripts, the volume printed in Greek with handsome characters engraved by Claude Garamond which reproduce the script of the Cretan Vergetios, the king's calligrapher. Two Latin versions appeared in the same year, and then the French one of Florent Chrestien in 1575. If you leaf through this text, you will feel yourself taken out of dates and history and transported into a universe which knows the alternation of night and day and the passing of seasons but is ignorant of the clock of centuries. Here is this world, at once older and younger than we, new at each dawn, which man has decimated and abused since the time of hunters in chlamydes or jerkins, who had at least the excuse of believing in the inexhaustible abundance of nature, an excuse we no longer have—we who not only continue to destroy animals but work to annihilate nature itself. Here is this world we rediscover with a beating heart every time we go for a walk at dawn and come upon a doe wandering at the woods' edge or fox cubs playing in the grass. Here is the paw or claw print on the sand, the water lapped up at dusk, the rut which joins savage, wild lovers in the forest. Here is the varied race of dogs; here is the tribe of horses, heroic and faithful vassals of man. Here is the innocent lion who quietly rips his prey to shreds; here is the erect stag, his extended neck protecting his herd, black in the pale dawn . . .

1955

15

A CIVILIZATION
IN WATERTIGHT
COMPARTMENTS

We have all gazed with horror and disgust at pictures by medieval painters or engravings of the seventeenth century which depict executions in public squares. Many of us have also, sick at heart, quickened our pace in some little town in Spain or in the Orient as we passed the local butcher shop with its flies, its still-warm carcasses, and its living animals tied up and trembling in front of the dead ones, the blood flowing in rivulets down the street. Our own civilization exists in watertight compartments: it protects us from such sights.

In La Villette, in channel number 2 of the new slaughterhouses, calves and bulls (the latter after a brutal drop) are hung up fully conscious before being killed, which enables the slaughter to proceed more quickly (time is money). To be sure, this system is illegal (under the terms of a law of April 16, 1964), but that doesn't prevent its being profitably employed nonetheless. The walls of our new slaughterhouses (splendid technical achievements, beyond any doubt, equipped with all the latest devices) are very thick: we do not see those creatures contorted with pain; we do not hear their bellows, which even the most ardent lover of steak would find intolerable. There is no danger that public conscience will affect digestion.

Oscar Wilde wrote somewhere that the worst crime of all is a lack of imagination: the human being has no feeling for evils he has not directly experienced or participated in. I have often thought that the sealed freight cars and the well-built walls of the concentration camps insured the extension and duration of crimes against humanity which would have been stopped sooner had they taken place in the open air and in full view. In the public squares of the Middle Ages and the Grand Siècle, habit surely numbed some of the spectators; yet there were always those who were affected by the sight, even if they did not protest loudly, and their whisperings were finally heard. The executioners of our day take better precautions.

"But look," exclaims the reader who is already irritated or amused (it takes little to amuse some readers), "we're talking about calves and cows, whose very names are ridiculous to the French, and you have the gall to speak of crimes against humanity in connection with them." Yes, I do: every act of cruelty experienced by thousands of living creatures is a crime against humanity, since it hardens and brutalizes humanity a little more. I'm afraid, alas, that it's not really within our possibilities as Frenchmen to stop the Vietnamese War immediately, to prevent the defoliation of Indochina, or to heal the wounds of India and Pakistan. Yet I do believe we can do something to stop quickly the nightmare of channel number 2 by using another channel, that of television. I am calling for a film filled with blood, bellowing, and genuine terror, which will perhaps give some sadists pleasure but will also produce a few thousand protests.

A few years ago I wrote the life of someone called Zeno, an imaginary character, of course, who refused to "digest death's agony." It is somewhat in his name that I have written these words.

1972

16

APPROACHES TO
TANTRISM

Lo Yoga della Potenza

Ｉt was in 1952 that I bought by chance in a bookshop in Florence, and in its original Italian, *Lo Yoga della Potenza* (*The Yoga of Power*), which was more intelligently translated into French some years later under the title *Yoga tantrique* [1971]. I didn't even know the author's name: Julius Evola. Apart from a few reservations which I shall mention later, I thereby acquired one of those works which continue to feed you over the years and which, to a certain degree, transform you.

Like many people in France, I had first glimpsed Tantrism through *Mystiques et magiciens du Tibet* by Alexandra David-Neel. Much later, the Hellenist and Orientalist Gabriel Germain, in that memoir of sorts of his mental life, *Le Regard intérieur* [1968] (a document too little read), indicated what he owed to this book which he first came upon when very young. An intelligent, daring woman intermingled with her tales of travel the account of a travelogue across strange frontiers. Whether one believes her on every point or not, she leads you as if by the hand to the rim of caverns which you feel that, had we ourselves dared explore them, we also should have discovered within ourselves. In the meantime, I had read a certain number of learned works on the subject. I had learned what differentiated Sivaist Tantrism from Buddhist Tantrism (the resemblances are greater than the differences); I knew more or less what a mandala, a mantra, and a mudra are, and some of the equivalences between the names of Hindu and Tibetan divinities. Evola's work, exceptionable though it seems to me in certain respects, brought me even more: the exposition of a method.

Others more qualified than I will reexamine Tantric Buddhism in its totality. In rough terms, we may say that it is concerned with a method of spiritual gymnastics built on the foundations of a psychology which can be considered a depth psychology and which, as is always the case, takes its support, whether consciously or not, from a metaphysic.

Surely one of the irreparable mistakes of the West has been to conceptualize the complex human substance under the antithetical form of body-soul and then to escape from this antithesis only by denying the soul. Another mistake, no less deplorable, and one that gets worse, consists in imagining the work of interior perfection or liberation only in terms of the development of the individual or person and not in the effacement of those two notions in favor of that of being or of what goes even further than being. Even more, it appears that, for the West, perfection and liberation are brutally opposed to each other instead of being represented as two faces of the same phenomenon. The study of Tantric Yoga tends to correct these errors, and that indicates the enormous profit a receptive reader can derive from a summa like that of Evola.

In contrast to what happens in Zen, where the *awakening* corresponds to a shock experienced suddenly, even though prepared for by a more or less lengthy wait, the Tantric awakening is progressive and the result of unceasing discipline. The adept must attain a maximum of *attention*, which itself is impossible without a maximum of serenity: a troubled surface does not reflect.

The prescriptions given by Evola, and the complex casuistry of causes and effects with which he accompanies them, seem to me of such importance, not only for the spiritual life but for the utilization of all the faculties, that I know of no human condition they cannot improve, whether it be that of the man of action, or that of the writer, or simply that of the man who gives himself to life. Those who know little of Tantrism are generally preoccupied with its erotic: Evola's detailed analysis demonstrates to what degree that is an integral part of a system which requires that one mobilize and discipline all his strength. But we are in the domain of the sacred, far from that of the sex shops.

The erotic procedures of Tantrism are not calculated, like those of the Tao, to ensure vigor and longevity to man, nor do they represent, like those of the Kama Sutra, a hygiene of fulfillment: they strive rather for a sacramental-ization of carnal union which the West has never known or wished to accept. It is a question of assimilating, through a series of successive interdictions and liberations, the plea-sure of a hierogamy, which is what it in effect is, but only on the condition that the lovers are aware of it. The slow, gradual familiarity achieved by means of looking, speaking, touching, and, ultimately, of physical cohabitation preced-ing carnal culmination, is hardly realizable for us except by a series of fortuitous chances and between two beings ca-pable of appreciating those moments of stopping as stages rather than as obstacles. In a world in which the liberation of sexual mores is not accompanied by a reevaluation of sensuality, but quite the contrary, at least to judge from the films, advertisements, and literature of our day, the Maithuma, the sacred coitus, is not likely to fall into the public domain.

To dispel certain misunderstandings, one must also speak of the phonemes (almost if not all of them Sanskrit mantras current in different sects of Hinduism and Buddhism) whose use is commended by Tantric masters. And to en-deavor to explain, even more, the use of unspoken phonemes, carved on stones at the expense of pilgrims or engraved on the rims of prayer wheels. For a Europe which has been severed from its ancient religious practices, such usages appear to be pure superstition. In part they are; but our age, in which political propaganda and the sale of commercial products are forced on the public with the aid of almost hypnotic slogans, would be wrong to fail to understand that the restoration of serenity, concentration, and both physical and mental liberation can equally well benefit from formulae which saturate the soul. An aged mutterer telling her beads doesn't cause us to experience the feeling of the sacred to any great degree; but remember that poetry, too, is made up of, or was made up of when it still recalled its magic origins, almost incantatory repetitions of sounds and rhythms. The interjection pure and simple and the oath or obscenity, often so worn away that its meaning is scarcely perceived, ease or calm the person who utters them, the way mantras do. We also know that in at least the first stage of control over the self the attentive repetition of a formula can stay the disordered flood of images which carry the mind away, but carry it nowhere.

Whoever has heard an officiant recite a Sanscrit mantra knows how it spreads out over the audience like concentric waves, enfolding the listener in the mystery of its sound. It used to be that way also with the Latin prayers of the Church, where the phenomenon of sound seemed to act *ex opere operato*. It is not for our time, when physics has made a science and a technology of vibrations, to deny the power of words spoken for themselves, that idea where the mantra joins the *Verbum* according to Saint John.

When confronted with techniques that have developed in a rich spiritual terrain different from our own, our first reaction is to reject them all, out of disdain and distrust for exoticism. The second, equally ill-fated, is to be attracted precisely by this exoticism. It is one of Evola's greatest merits that he combines a prodigious wealth of erudite detail with the gift of isolating from their local conditioning the ideas or disciplines that are of value for us, thus doing away with the very idea of exoticism. Like Jung's preface to *Bardo Thodol*, which surveys an analogous subject from far above, the work of Evola on Tantric Yoga and that, almost as valuable, which he has devoted to the medieval Hermetic tradition is at least superficially oriented in the same direction as modern psychology, but with several essential differences which Jung noted and which Evola would like to proclaim loudly.

Because of his insistence on its mental disciplines, his study of Tantric Yoga is especially salubrious in a time when all discipline is naïvely discredited. At the same time, thanks to his lucid analysis of the *living* content of a ritual—and of the myths to which this ritual refers (I am thinking in particular of the visualization of secondary divinities and of visions from beyond the tomb)—this book and several others by scholars who have worked in the same area give us the possibility of adhering to our own rituals and myths, a possibility which the strict rationalism at the beginning of the century seemed to have eliminated forever.

My own study of Tantrism has brought me closer to, rather than further away from, Christian thought. Neither has it taken me away from what is today more or less confusingly called humanism, not merely because the precision and discriminating logic of Tantric prescriptions are essentially intellectual, but also because to try to understand and control those forces which are within us is never contrary to the notion of humanism.

The Tantric method is psychological and not ethical: it urges us to retain our strengths, not to acquire virtues. It is that which has resulted in grave misunderstandings.

In fact—and Proust noted this phenomenon with his usual acuity—almost all the virtues, even goodness, are primarily virtues of *energy*. Beyond that, there are forces as liberated as electricity, which can electrocute someone or light his room. Tantric Yoga is a level beyond Hindu Yoga, possessing as well, in Tibet, certain shamanist elements. In every case its metaphysic takes it beyond both non-dualistic Hinduism and Buddhism, which teaches detachment from and compassion towards other beings. Every diversion of strength acquired by means of mental disciplines at the expense of greed, pride, and desire for power does not annul those forces, whether they are normal or, *in one way or another*, supranormal, but rather causes them to fall back ipso facto into a world where every action has consequences and where every excess of strength turns back on its possessor. That is a law from which nothing escapes and which we have seen exercised in the realm of technological powers, themselves indifferent to good and evil but destructive the minute they are placed in the hands of human greed. At the center of the mental disciplines of Buddhism, as at the center of the Christian mystique, the state of detachment and clarity which is achieved renders almost unthinkable every utilization of power exercised by a baneful egotism.

And it is on this matter that Evola's work, so obsessed with pure power, calls up certain reservations. Who was this man who transmitted to us the essentials of the Tibetan Tantric experience only a few years before political cataclysms reduced that tradition to the precarious state of dissidence and exile? The few details I have gleaned from people who knew him are not verifiable, even though they correspond to the character traits his books reveal here and there.

Like Malaparte, Evola seems to have belonged to that type of Germanized Italian in which some undefinable Ghibeline obsessions survive. He is one of those whom the *Revolt against the Modern World* (that is the title of another of his books), however justified it may be in part, led into even more dangerous latitudes than those they believed they were leaving.

As in the works of Stefan George or in the *Frederick II*

of Kantorowicz, one encounters early on in his books a dream of aristocratic and sacerdotal domination, for which there is no proof that it ever corresponded to some Golden Age in the past and of which, in our own day, we have seen only grotesque and frightful caricatures. In the less balanced works of Evola, the concept of a chosen race (which in practice leads straight to racism) is combined with an almost morbid greed for supranormal powers, which causes him to accept unabashedly the most material aspects of the spiritual adventure.

This regrettable passage from the notion of intellectual and mystical powers to the notion of simple power itself stains some of his pages and especially some of his conclusions in his great book on Tantric Yoga.* This singular bias in a scholar of genius in no way diminishes his astonishing special gifts, which were to transmit and to comment. Yet it is clear that Baron Julius Evola, who was ignorant of no aspect of the great Tantric tradition, never dreamed of arming himself with that secret weapon of Tibetan lamas, the Dagger-for-killing-the-Self.

1972

---

* The original title, *Lo Yoga della Potenza*, clearly indicates this innate tendency of the author, who always seems somewhat closer to the sorcerer than to the mystic.

17

WRITTEN
IN A GARDEN

Color is the expression of a hidden virtue.

. . .

Some birds are flames.

. . .

A gardener caused me to notice that it is in autumn that one perceives the true color of trees. In the spring, the abundance of chlorophyll gives them all a livery of green. Once September has come, they reveal themselves garbed in their specific colors, the blond, golden birch, the yellow-orange-red maple, the oak, color of bronze and of iron.

. . .

Nothing has helped me more to understand natural phenomena than the two Hermetic signs which signify air and water and which then, when crossed with a bar which in some way slows up their force, symbolize fire—less free, tied to ligneous matter or fossil oil—and earth with its heavy, soft particles. The tree includes all four in its hieroglyph. Fastened to the earth, drenched with air and water, it nevertheless mounts to the sky like a flame; it is a green flame before it one day ends as a red flame in fireplaces, in forest fires, or at the martyr's stake. By its vertical thrust, it belongs to the world of forms that rise; like water, which nourishes it, to those forms that, left to themselves, fall to earth.

.   .   .

Hermetic sign of air: an empty triangle pointing upward. On calm days, the green pyramid of the tree holds itself in the air in perfect balance. On windy days, the agitated branches sketch out the beginnings of a flight.

.   .   .

Water, which of itself gives way and falls. And that is why the Franciscan adjective for it is so appropriate: *umile.*

.   .   .

What is more beautiful than that statue by Rodin of a suppliant in which the man who is praying holds up his arms and extends them like the branches of a tree? Indubitably, the tree prays to the divine light.

.   .   .

Roots buried in earth, branches protecting the squirrels' games and the birds' nest and chirpings, shade bestowed on man and beast, head in heaven. Is there a wiser, more beneficent mode of existing?

.   .   .

And from there to the involuntary start of revulsion at the presence of the woodman and the far greater horror of the chain saw. To bring low and kill what cannot flee.

.   .   .

The miracle of snapshots which fix the image of spurting water, jetting upward, rebounding on high, like the spray of foam from a wave broken on the edge of a boulder. The dead wave gives birth to this great white ghost which in an instant will cease to exist. At the click of a shutter, the heavy water rises like smoke, like vapor, like a soul.

.　　.　　.

For an inverse reason, the exquisite, artificial beauty of the fountain. Hydraulics oblige the water to behave like a flame, to renew ceaselessly within its liquid column its ascent to heaven. The forced water rises to the apogee of the fluid obelisk before regaining its liberty, which is to fall.

.　　.　　.

All water aspires to vapor; all vapor becomes water again.

.　　.　　.

Ice. Sparkling immobility. Pure condensation. Stable water.

.　　.　　.

I consider the landscapes of certain fjords of Alaska and Norway in springtime among the most ravishing, when water simultaneously appears in its three forms and in various aspects. The shivering but slack water of the fjord, the streaming water of cascades on vertical walls of rock, the vapor that rises from their fall, the water in the form of cloud which traces a route to the sky, the frost and snow of the nearby summits which spring has not yet ascended.

.　　.　　.

Composite rock, formed of volcanic lava and sediment borne by water, an amalgam thousands of centuries old. And their exterior form perpetually reworked, resculpted by air and water.

.　　.　　.

Your body, composed three-quarters of water plus a few terrestrial minerals, a small handful. And this great flame within you, whose nature you do not comprehend. And within your lungs, captured and recaptured continuously within the thoracic cage, air, that lovely stranger without whom you cannot live.

1980

18

TRIBUTES

In Memory of Diotima:

Jeanne de Vietinghoff

To Mme Hélène Naville

There are souls who make us believe the soul exists.
They are not always the most genial: the most genial are
those who can best express themselves. Sometimes they are
babbling souls; often they are silent souls. Jeanne de Vietinghoff, who died recently, left several books. Some of
them are very beautiful.* They present, however, only an
etiolated image of the woman herself—and even the most
beautiful portraits do not replace the dead. The books of
Jeanne de Vietinghoff, for those who knew her, give a simple commentary on the poem that was her life. Inspired by
reality, they remain inferior to it; they are no more than
the ashes of a splendid fire. I should like to enable those
who did not know her to feel the intimate warmth of those
ashes.

I should like to put aside everything that is merely an
envelope, an appearance, a surface, in order to go directly
to the heart of this rose, to the bottom of this sweet chalice.
Let me say simply, for that will explain certain things, that

* La Liberté intérieure, l'intelligence du bien, 7th and 8th editions. Au Seuil d'un
monde nouveau, 1921, 2nd edition. Sur l'Art de Vivre, 1923. Impressions d'âme, 4th
edition. L'Autre devoir, a novel, is a rather more mediocre book.

Jeanne de Vietinghoff was born a Protestant. She never broke with that faith, which she accepted from childhood; she was not one of those who break with things easily. "What one believes matters little," she said; "what matters is *how* one believes." We can learn from this exceptional woman how to disengage ourselves from the external forms in which we enclose God. The higher we rise, the more we hold sway over our beliefs. Ultimately, Jeanne de Vietinghoff came more and more to belong to that invisible church, without a name or dogmas, in which all sincerities live in communion.

For her, truth was not some fixed point, but an ascending line. The truth of today, fashioned out of a renouncement of yesterday's truth, would give way in advance before future truths. Each truth—and she accepted all of them—was for her only a road which ought to lead higher. "What today seems to me the principal thing will tomorrow be only an accessory. My ideal of perfection varies; sometimes I attribute it to obedience, sometimes to grandeur, sometimes to discipline, sometimes to the sincerity of my life. I ask what is the number and what is the value of the virtues, and yet it is always the same God I obey, with an equally sincere heart." The indefatigable impetus of a soul always en route: this mystical way of life is nothing but a perpetual departure.

Everything slips away. The soul assists, motionless, at the passing of joys, of sorrows, of deaths, out of which it composes a life. She had been given "the great lesson of things that pass away." It took her a long time to recognize, within that changing décor, the intimate, unwavering line of interior development. She had groped her way through all things; she had made passions her transitory mirror. "Men who have wished to embellish the soul have thought they should decorate it with beliefs and principles, the way they adorn the saints in their sanctuaries with precious stones and gold; but the soul is only beautiful when it is naked . . ." At moments she manages to perceive herself in her eternal shape. I would suggest to readers of Tagore that they copy these lines of Jeanne de Vietinghoff into the margin of *Gitanjali*:

Everything I see seems to me a reflection, everything I hear a distant echo, and my soul searches for the wondrous source, for it thirsts for pure water.

The centuries pass, and the world wears away, but my soul is always young; it keeps its vigil among the stars, in the night of time.

Jeanne de Vietinghoff wrote the poem of life, of life which does not pass away as those who live do.

Mme de Vietinghoff was suspicious of virtues painfully achieved; she wanted them to be spontaneous, happy. "Why make a chore of life when one can make a smile of it?" She wanted her virtues to be natural, the way all things are. She understood, better than I can say, the infinite diversity of nature, which leads each soul, each mind, each body down divergent roads to the same goal of happiness. This accessible soul was an accepting soul.

Do not judge. Life is a mystery, and each of us obeys different laws. Do you know the power of the things that led them, what sufferings and desires furrowed their road? Have you come upon the voice of their conscience, which reveals to them in whispers the secret of their destiny? Do not judge: consider the pure lake and tranquil waters at which the thousand waves which sweep across the universe finally arrive . . . Everything you behold must arrive there. All the waves of the ocean are required to bear the ship of truth to port.

Believe in the efficacy of the death of all you wish for, in order to take your part in the triumph of what must be.

Reading these words, one cannot doubt that Jeanne de Vietinghoff had a heart of genius.

For the wise man, grief is not a redemption but an evolution. "One has to have exhausted one's grief before one can reach that tranquil hour which precedes the new dawn." In her life, which was not without shadows but was always without blemish, Jeanne de Vietinghoff unfailingly kept herself at the level of happiness. To renounce happiness, or to discourage others from it, was to her an inexcusable fault. No doubt, "whenever it encounters a being of good-will, life undertakes, by causing him to experience the insufficiency of what is mediocre, to elevate his idea of happiness." Suffering, like joy, was for her a passerby who finally spoke of other things.

Yet it is imprudent to disdain too quickly. The soul who is mistress of herself rejects no pleasure, even those considered vulgar; she tastes it, possesses it, and one day goes beyond it. "Sometimes I think that if death were to come to me unexpectedly before I had soaked myself completely in the river of life, I would say to him: go away; the hour has not yet struck . . . The repose of Thy great blue heaven would crush me if I still possessed so much as one strength I had not yet spent, and Thy eternal felicity would be mingled with regret if there were one flower left on earth whose perfume I had not smelled." Here, in this ardor and in this detachment, I also hear the pulsing fever of the young André Gide.

When Diotima undertook to explain God to the banqueters of the *Symposium*, she condemned no form of human passion but endeavored merely to attach it to the infinite. It did not bother her to see the guests at that banquet tarrying on the earthly roadway; if necessary, she could have traveled it herself. "The greatest earthly happiness leads only to the border of heaven." She knows that life, or perhaps death, will always lead us to our goal in the end, and that that goal is God.

It is we who are not ready. The objects of our contentment have been there for days, for years, possibly for centuries; they wait for the light to enter our eyes so that we may see them and for the strength to come into our arms that we may seize them. They await, puzzled to be there such a long time useless.

We suffer, she also said, *we suffer each time we doubt someone or something, but our suffering is transformed into joy the moment we have embraced, in that person or in that thing, the immortal beauty which caused us to love them.*

No doubt. Blindness, far from increasing our ability to love, narrows the space in which our love has free play. Perhaps Plato spoke the truth, and Jeanne de Vietinghoff was right.

Lives may be beautiful because of different qualities, through their surrender or through their steadfastness. There are melodic lives, just as there are sculptural lives. Only music—a Bach fugue or a Mozart sonata—seems to me to express so much fervor, serenity, and ease.

Not what is seen or said or thought, but the unrelenting union which unites, beyond all sentient things, my joy with yours in whatever is inexpressible in our souls.

Not vows or kisses or caresses, but the rhythmic harmony in universal growth . . .

Her penultimate book, which was perhaps inspired by Count Kayserling,* brings a generous audacity to the study of the problems of the years after the war. Jeanne de Vietinghoff offers the world the method of salvation she proposed for individual souls: a perpetual transmutation of values, not abrupt but progressive. "Be patient while you wait, for fear lest you seize upon a transitory form . . . Have you, then, so little faith that you cannot live one hour without religion, without morality, without philosophy?" In 1925, Mme de Vietinghoff did not despair of our cre-

* See note at end.

puscular Europe. The coming generation seemed to her to bear within it "the triumph of human strength"—that is, I believe, of sincerity. These excessive hopes seem to me like some form of maternal love: Jeanne de Vietinghoff believed in youth and in the future of the world, because she had two sons. It is doubtless that which moves me so much in this beautiful book: I like the loving woman in her even more than the sibyl.

She always doubted that man would have to answer for what are called his sins. She thought they were like those shards of marble which accumulate around an unfinished masterpiece in the sculptor's studio—inevitable debris. Continuing the same line of thought, we may suppose that she might have believed our virtues are not meritorious: that would have been, on her part, evidence of humility. In the last years of her life, looking at her weary but undiscouraged hands, Mme de Vietinghoff was gently surprised at the courage their gestures indicated. She thought she had lived her life as an irresponsible spectator, merely consenting. In the end, she came to prefer, above everything, this simplicity of empty hands. She, too, appears to have stripped herself in order to sleep:

O God, I would that each morning as I look up to Thee I might offer Thee my empty hands.

I would, rather than make an effort, be nothing more than a receptacle of the wave of infinitude and travel down roads by chance, urged on only by the breath of inner voices.

I would forget my wisdom and my reasons, ask nothing more, cease all desiring, and accept with a smile the roses Thy hand lets fall in my lap.

> *Odors of things we have not acquired,*
> *Sweetness of undeserved happinesses,*
> *Beauty of truths our thought has not created . . .*

I have neglected to say how beautiful she herself was. She was still almost young when she died, before the trials of old age came, which she did not fear. Much more than her writing, it is her life which gives me the impression of perfection. For there is something much rarer than competence, talent, or even genius, and that is nobility of soul. Had Jeanne de Vietinghoff written nothing, her character would be no less lofty. Only, many of us would never have known it. It is the way of the world that the rarest virtues of a person always remain the secret of someone else.

Thus did this Platonic life unfold. Jeanne de Vietinghoff unceasingly evolved from everyday wisdom to a higher wisdom, from the indulgence that excuses to the indulgence that understands, from a love of life to that love, utterly disinterested, which life inspired in her, and—as she herself put it—"from the loving God of little children to the infinite Deity of the sage." Perhaps those theosophical dreams, like strange but amicable visions, which one sees when one closes one's eyes to sleep, also came to console her at the approach of evening. Life on earth, which she loved so much, was for her only the visible side of life eternal. No doubt she accepted death as a night darker than the others, but one which would be followed by a more shining dawn. One would like to believe she was not mistaken. One would like to believe that the dissolution in the tomb did not arrest such a rare development; one would like to believe that death, for such souls, is merely one further step.

.   .   .

N O T E : *From a literary point of view, we should remember that the Baronne de Vietinghoff, Dutch by birth, belonged by her marriage to that Baltic family from which came Barbe-Julie de Vietinghoff, the Baronne de Krudner, and the mystical counselor of Czar Alexander. These two foreigners spoke in French. Also, Baron de Vietinghoff has told me that* Au Seuil d'un monde nouveau *was in no way inspired by the German philosopher Kayserling. I use this note to make this small correction.*

1929

Sketch for a Portrait
of Jean Schlumberger

I was twenty-four years old when, one bitter cold Swiss spring day, the Countess of Bylandt, a Dutch friend who knew Jean Schlumberger, gave me more or less in confidence his account of the last months of his wife's life; it was a masterpiece of gravity, of self-control, and yet of unutterable emotion in the face of the death of another person, which Schlumberger himself only consented to make public many years later. At that time, I was living from day to day through a similar experience, and I had just heard the echoes of yet another such experience, which had happened very recently. The book touched me deeply, as I am sure Jean Schlumberger wished to touch the reader, and gave me a lesson in lucidity and courage. Of all the works he has left us, I don't know any more perfect than this stoic, puritan tribute which, much later, enabled him to look down on (in my opinion, perhaps somewhat unjustly) André Gide's *Et nunc manet in te*, which is also devoted more or less confidentially to the memory of a wife who had died.

Having entered thus abruptly into the very heart of the work of a great writer of whom I knew nothing, not even his name, I subsequently read other things: *Les Yeux de dix-huit ans* first, and especially *Le Dialogue avec le corps endormi*, which corresponded too closely to my own preoccupations not to have become for me a milestone or roadmark on the paths I was later to travel and retravel. Somewhat later, I read *La Mort de Sparte*, inadequately appreciating at first its gnarled beauty, its harsh and almost rustic texture substituting for the smooth, skillfully dressed marble of Plutarch; yet it remains among the most noble texts inspired by antiquity in our time. Although I went no further, I had read enough to know that my relations with Jean Schlumberger would never be those instantaneous and violent relationships one has with certain authors who embody in themselves the passions and predilections of an age, whom one rejects, then accepts, then rejects again only to accept ultimately on another level. From the very first, he established himself as an unquestionable value—one of those values which can wait.

It was around 1930 in a Parisian salon that I met for the first time this quick, dry man with a courtesy that no longer exists. It did not, properly speaking, constitute an entering into contact with him, I imagine he scarcely noticed my presence, which, in any case, was insignificant. He had just come back from Braffy, where he said he had spent many hours trimming his yews (or was it his box?). "Trimming his yews is what he's done far too often," muttered someone skeptically. I did not agree with that criticism. I loved those avenues of French gardens which stretched behind Jean Schlumberger. A great deal later, when I had read *Saint-Saturnin*, I understood the almost tragic poetry that arises from his work out of those beautiful plantings that are so quickly ravaged, often by the same people who set them out. In that novel, which is constructed like an oratorio, voices from different ages of life alternate, but always overpowered by the muffled rumbling of old age with its crackings like those of a dead tree.* It is striking that a man who was to experience, and experience with great happiness, a very old age should have twice depicted vividly its constraints and dangers, in the William of *Saint-Saturnin* and in the Retz of *Le Lion devenu vieux*.

Moreover, it is characteristic of him that both times he placed these images of confusion in an almost majestically traditional framework: for Retz, the society of the age of Louis XIV, apparently controlled to excess; for *Saint-Saturnin*, the rather austere dignity of the home of important members of the Protestant, provincial bourgeoisie. In both cases, one may suppose that for many readers who are only half attentive the heavily molded or carved frame may have caused them somewhat to forget about the portraits themselves, and that those elements which sometimes make one think of the art of Champaigne, sometimes of that of Rigaud, may have obscured those gleams of Rembrandt which shine from out of the heart of the book.

When I returned to Paris in 1951, communications were definitively established between Jean Schlumberger and me, and we were able to engage in deep conversations. I recall especially one of his questions about Hadrian, whose portrait I had just endeavored to sketch: "Did Hadrian judge himself?" I could have answered, borrowing a phrase from my own book, that inasmuch as he was a jurist, Hadrian was quite aware of the difficulty of judging. "Hadrian meditates extensively on his own life." "Yes, but does he *judge* himself?" I understood the differences between us: the Pur-

---

* From the point of view of musical construction alone, it has probably not yet been noted that his charming *Quatre Potiers*, located like *Saint-Saturnin* in the Normandy countryside, makes of this book a fitting counterpart to operetta. The young voices in it predominate over the rough but benevolent voice of an old man. Nonetheless, this rather rosy novel also contains a scene of startling blackness: the suicide of the schoolboy, whose convention-bound family disguise his death as an accident. A respectful member of the haute bourgeoisie, down to the last proprieties of his class, Schlumberger—like Martin Du Gard and quite as much as Gide—knew what lay underneath bourgeois realities.

itan humanist needed to have his characters sit in judgment on what I would call their own assizes, yet is ready to show them often acquitting themselves, as the hero of *Un Homme heureux* does. For me, the characters of the drama were, rather, both objects and subject, both experimenters and the results of experiments, the accomplices and witnesses, rather than the judges, of their own destinies. I am persuaded that they were also more like that in Schlumberger than he wanted to admit. The father in *Saint-Saturnin* is on that disquieting borderline where senile idiocy and the most cold-eyed lucidity join to achieve the goal of domestic tyranny; the happy man of the book of that title seems to believe the reasons he gives himself for leaving his family and then for returning to them, but we clearly feel that there are others he doesn't express and that the author would not be distressed to have us go beyond the limits his prudence imposed on him. There are more mirror-games than one might suppose in these works which at first glance appear like those orderly, bare rooms of austere bourgeois elegance in certain Dutch paintings (and one can't avoid thinking of his de Witte ancestors). But when one looks at them more closely, these rooms reveal that they are imbued with the secret lives of their inhabitants and of those who have preceded them within these walls; and a window left carefully ajar, sometimes seen only in a mirror that reflects it, causes the out-of-doors to penetrate into that interior.

In the great collection of his *Oeuvres complètes*, which he was happily able to put in order before he died, I seem especially drawn to reread the "portraits": the portraits of the Guizot and Schlumberger families in *Souvenirs*; the portraits of friends and colleagues in the chronicles he did for the *N.R.F.* and with extracts from which he chronologically joined together, as it were, his books; and also the depictions of actions, events, and the currents of ideas in the political observations he made between 1938 and 1945, which will be exceedingly valuable to future analysts. In these assured

sketches, never overstated and often playful, though never
to the point of being ironic, we find his perpetual concern
to make judgments. A concern which at first seems to be
the opposite of Gide's *Ne jugez pas*; yet we recognize that
the two points of view are really one: for Gide is protesting
against the hasty response of preconceived opinions, against
judgments made *in advance*. Above all, Schlumberger in-
sists, as much in the psychological as in the social sphere,
on the unending necessity of measuring, of weighing, and
of taking one's bearing without being carried away by cross-
currents. Not the golden mean, as he somewhere has one
of his characters call it, knowing that one can get that wrong,
but rather, in terms borrowed from Taoist wisdom, whose
principles he knew well, the true mean.

But I do not want to conclude without insisting on this
phrase, which may appear, wrongly, to describe an ambition that was almost too modest.* In his *Oeuvres complètes*,
the essay "On the Frontiers of Religion" rejoins those
daring meditations of the man confronted with his own
sleeping body from the great *Dialogue avec le corps endormi*.
More important, he goes beyond those meditations in his
total and active acceptance, by means of the intelligence,
of what goes beyond intelligence itself. In their depths,
these two works open up perspectives down avenues of
carefully trimmed yews which give on not only desolate,
stoic landscapes (as in *Saint-Saturnin*) but the dizzying spaces
of the void as well. It appears that the characteristically
cautious bearing of Jean Schlumberger was more useful than
harmful to his true freedom: his puritan rigor, which, according to him, was mitigated rather late in life but never
rejected, for many years gave him a sort of gluttonous desire
to live as a discreet presence in his books—a quality which

---

* "There are certain Chinese maxims which are like water that appears to be
pure but which twists your bowels," he says, more or less, somewhere. I cite it
here without being able to refer to the book.

stands in contrast to Gide's more hectic avidity.* His Protestant activism and rationalism on the one hand and his humanism on the other, rather than keeping him out of certain areas, helped him to live at ease in an inner world, especially in that of the masters of Asian wisdom, which the average Frenchman, skeptical by nature, doesn't often enter and probably entered even less often in his day than in ours. As always, and for every writer, but especially for those who are subject by necessity or by nature to the most strict control, it is his passing remarks or the observations he made under his breath that are the most important ones to listen to; they inform us about lands their proprietor has not invited us to visit, situated, as it were, beyond his gates and sea-walls. If you listen to him carefully, it sometimes seems that this man, who almost voluntarily withdrew from our generation and even from his own, nevertheless advanced bolder propositions than many of his contemporaries who were thought to be more adventurous than he.

1969

---

* All of which was not without a certain charming frivolousness in Jean's old age. I think it delighted him to be a descendant of that minister of Louis-Phillipe who was also the lover of the Princess de Lieven; and our very last conversation, if I remember correctly, had much to do with the charms of ballerinas' faces and legs.

Tribute to Jacques Masui

In the true sense of the word *know*, I have known Jacques Masui since 1953, when his collection of texts on Yoga came into my hands. That was the moment when my reading in the area of Oriental wisdom, which I had been doing in an intermittent way since my youth, began to cease being a mere subject of study and became instead a clearly marked influence on my life. His *Yoga* was a signpost at the beginning of a road on which I was to travel much further. It was characteristic of Masui—and probably of a whole type of person at once generous, prudent, and modest—to express himself above all in collecting or in elucidating the writings of someone else, to make himself the conduit through which the water from the sources can reach us.

His work will not really be accessible to the public until we have collected in one volume the *Réflexions préliminaires*, the *Commentaires*, and the *Réflexions finales* which he discreetly placed at the head or at the end of issues of the review *Hermès* (which was in fact his life's work), his *Préfaces* to the works in the "Collection spirituelle," which he directed for the publisher Fayard, and his anthology *De la vie intérieure*, a florilegium of texts devoted to the mystical experience but here especially to those of Western origin. The selection goes from Daumal to Milosz, and the texts assembled contain the essentials one should know about the methods of spiritual progress, which many people denigrate without having learned about them and which others, who become intoxicated with them, often know only in inauthentic forms.

We had been corresponding with each other for some time when I went to wait for him—four years ago, I believe—at a small airport near the island on which I live. I later learned that the tossing of the little plane and the badly regulated atmospheric pressure had given him a painful otitis which afflicted him throughout the few days he spent here. I remember him as a robust man, tall, with a physiognomy which had something Oriental about it. "Belgians look like the Japanese," Giraudoux said paradoxically; but with Jacques Masui that look came, above all, from a sort of imperturbable tranquillity. From the very first moment, we were friends.

A few days later, we underwent the test of one of those little trials which bring together those who experience them, allowing them better to judge one another. We were trying to visit an aged American who had lived in Japan, had become a genuine Zen master, and had come to live on a farm in a quite isolated region, where he still is known for teaching farming and Oriental wisdom to the young people of Maine with good results. Jacques Masui had known him well in Paris, then in Tokyo, and he still retained a pious image of this student of Zen. But this terribly busy contemplative would not receive us, despite an appointment which had been made in advance and the repeated messages we had sent him through some of his disciples. We saw him from afar, working in the fields. It was a very hot spring day; we passed part of the time we waited picnicking in the shade of an abandoned barn. As we went home, we debated to what extent a sage could and should refuse contacts with others: unquestionably, these delays were the equivalent of an initiatory test; in former times, masters sometimes obliged new arrivals to wait for days, or even weeks, in the snow, and one pious suppliant became famous for having cut off his arm to prove his sincerity. We did not go that far. Yet Jacques Masui was not just any suppliant for this Zen master; and I feel sure he thought, as I did, that the true sage is he who can easily leave his contemplation (ecstasy or, as one might call it, intasy—satori or sadhana) and the manual tasks which at times accompany it in order to respond to even some banal remark of a passerby, but even more to greet a friend, and then sink back into that inner world which, in fact, he has never left. There is no wisdom without courtesy, no sanctity without human warmth.

Jacques Masui's goodwill towards me was soon subjected to a formidable trial. Without warning, he asked me to participate in a work on Tantrism for which he had to assemble original texts and commentaries in a very short time. I was imprudent enough to say yes, since I owed much to Tantric methods of attention and concentration; but at the very first sentences of my essay I realized that it would take me another six months of thought and study. Caught short, I turned out one of those hasty papers which are falsified by all that isn't said and in which the strain to present difficult ideas ends up, paradoxically, in superficiality. He accepted my work even though he judged it, I'm sure, as harshly as I did.*

Asia did not provide our only meeting ground. We discovered ancestors who must have rubbed elbows in the Brussels of other times; he had lived for a while during his youth at Marchienne, whence my mother's family takes its name. We dined together at the home of an American colonel who had been born in France, had been brought up in Austria, and had parachuted not long before into the maquis

---

* The essay "Approaches to Tantrism" in the present volume is a reworking of that first attempt.

with a French passport; we compared our memories of those difficult years. I took the usual walk up the mountain and drive along the seaside corniche with him. More than once, he later spoke to me of a second visit he wished to make to what he called "that Paradise." But all Paradises are within: into that corner of Maine he had doubtless brought his own. That project was never realized: I learned of his death in a newspaper article. With the greatest discretion, in the letters he wrote me before his death, he never once made any allusion to the illness he must already have had. And here I would also give thought to his wife, whom I did not know but of whom he spoke often, and who made the noble gesture of not surviving him.

We met also in our interest in the work, then still new, of Castaneda, half ethnologist, half novelist, which attempted to present the world view of a Yaqui magus. After Mircea Eliade's great book on shamanism, which had transformed our ideas about primitive mentality in its affinities with the sacred, we enjoyed this reconstruction (which was certainly in part factitious yet also alive and three-dimensional) of a form of mental activity which goes back to prehistory.

I had more time than our friend did to observe the increasingly obvious falsehoods and the great moments, which were underscored, as it were, with organ diapasons the way they are in films, accumulate in the subsequent works of Castaneda; the first magus was soon accompanied by a second, to comic effect, who formed with him a tandem that ended up resembling nothing so much as two of the Marx Brothers. For a long time, Jacques Masui was more indulgent than I: he accepted that the author should use what means he could to disseminate what he so perfectly described as "this ontological wisdom"; nevertheless, the image of the Yaqui magus in a jacket discoursing on his art in a good Mexican restaurant was already shocking to this man so insistent on exactitude. These reservations did not prevent us from admiring those superb pages in which the ethnography, more and more burdened with fiction, was at times impregnated with pure poetry: that "Voyage to Ixlan," for example, in the volume of the same name, worthy of figuring among the finest allegories of the earthly pilgrimage which have come down to us from the Middle Ages, or that description of the automobile headlights which two men traveling at night on the lonely roads of Mexico see intermittently in their rear-view mirror and which the Yaqui identifies as Death's: "Death is always following us, but it doesn't always turn on its headlights." Those of Jacques Masui's death were closer than we realized.

To stay with this subject, which is not inappropriate for a commemorative essay: we differed concerning the passage in which Castaneda incongruously has his Mexican magus read a translation of the *Bardo Thodel*, the Tibetan Book of the Dead, in which the aged Indian declares that he sees an allegory of life, not death. Jacques Masui agreed: that floating, that passage, and that alternation of terror and beatitude seemed to him to resemble more the successive states of our present life than what occurs (or doesn't occur) after it. But, just as dreams are made of the same substance as daily life, only organized differently, it may be that the contents of death and of life resemble each other and that such a discussion was merely academic. As for me, I remain disposed to believe that the Tibetan text ought to be accepted literally, as concerning the states after death, preceded as they are by the admirable, clinical description of dying. In fact, these great objurgations of the lamas addressing the defunct are strangely similar to those of the Catholic liturgy ("Leave this world, O Christian soul . . ." "Quit this flesh, O noble dead one . . ."). In the Tibetan as in the Christian, one seems to feel both the ancient concern to prevent the ghost from haunting the living and the pious desire to assist the soul in leaving its ruined home and accustoming itself to its new state of weightlessness.

Now Jacques Masui knows more than we do on this subject, unless, from that point of view, death is like life and we are living it without knowing what it is.

1976

Translator's Note

Although the publisher has chosen to defer its appearance until now, this translation of *Le Temps, ce grand sculpteur* was completed more than four years ago, some months before Marguerite Yourcenar's death on December 18, 1987. During the spring and again in the late summer of that year, she spent many hours reviewing the manuscript with me; but in those final months of ill health and personal grief, she tired quickly and was easily distracted, so that our conversations devoted to this English version often strayed onto an unbounded terrain of countless other subjects, literary, historical, philosophical, poetic, and personal. As a result, this manuscript never received quite the meticulous attention she gave my translations of her fiction, and it is, I fear, the poorer for that.

Yet I am infinitely the richer for our prolonged talks about both this book's language and its ranging subject matter. To discuss the dilemmas of translation with Marguerite Yourcenar was to be shown unnoticed subtleties in both languages; to wander off with her into the worlds of Greece and Rome, India and Spain, Japan and the Low Countries, medieval England and Renaissance Italy, all of which are encompassed in these essays, was to receive an incomparable education. What I recall most fondly, however, is the intimacy we shared on those long Galsworthian afternoons in the garden at Petite Plaisance and our companionable evenings by the fireside, her scrupulosity in striving for the most accurate possible rendering not only of meaning but also of tone, her generous encouragement, and her unfailing empathy.

During that summer, she was enthusiastically preoccupied with the lecture on Jorge Luis Borges I had invited her to give at Harvard in the coming autumn. That noble tribute was to become the last thing she wrote. The two of us had chatted with Borges at length several years earlier, on the evening before he and she were both awarded honorary degrees at Harvard, and she had been one of the very last persons to visit him before his death in Switzerland the previous spring. We were both, I know, conscious of the presence of his spirit as we alternately labored over this translation and discussed his writings during those sunlit days in Maine. By then, I had learned that I would be moving to Italy the following year, and she was filled with anticipatory delight at the prospect of coming to spend the winter and spring of 1989 with me in Florence, which she had not visited for some years. Such reminiscences—what Victor Hugo terms (in the splendid poem from which this collection of essays takes its title) "the muted whisper of blurred memories"—nostalgically assail me now, as I prepare to turn the final version of this text over to the printer, with a suffusing sense of both fulfillment and loss.

I had, in fact, never meant to translate this particular book and did so, at her request, only to please her. But then, I have never actually intended to translate anything for publication, the few renderings I have published from Modern Greek and French having all come about more or less by chance and always as an act of homage. In every case, I have been able to devote to these undertakings "onelye [as Sir Thomas More once charmingly put it] that tyme, wyche I steale from slepe and meate." And yet, few pastimes have proved more engrossing or more rewarding.

My memories of evenings spent translating this book are closely interwoven with inexpressibly joyful memories of my beloved son and daughter at that time. When I embarked on this translation, they were still children; by now, they are young adults.

"Happy is the man who is lucky in his children," proclaims a chorus of Euripides; and I can only say that it is hard for me to imagine that any father has been luckier than I. Marguerite Yourcenar, who followed my children's lives with unflagging interest and involvement, admired them both with great affection. It is, therefore, to David and Miranda that I dedicate this translation, *pro plurimis parvulum*, out of immense pride and measureless love, in the hope that their lives may continue to reflect the spirit of inquiry and learning, tolerance and freedom, understanding and charity, expressed in these pages.

W.K.

I Tatti
Florence
March 4, 1991

Bibliographical Note

BY YVON BERNIER

1. "On Some Lines from the Venerable Bede": *Nouvelle Revue française* 280 (April 1976), 1–7. *Without change.*
2. "Sistine": *Revue bleue* 22 (Nov. 21, 1931), 684–87.
3. "Tone and Language in the Historical Novel": *Nouvelle Revue française* 238 (Oct. 1972), 101–23. *Without change.*
4. "That Mighty Sculptor, Time": *Revue des voyages* 15 (Dec. 1954), 6–9. Reprinted in *Voyages* (Paris: Olivier Orban, 1981), pp. 181–85. *Without change.*
5. "On a Dream of Dürer's": *Hamsa* (second of two issues devoted to "L'Esotérisme d'Albrecht Dürer), 1977, pp. 42–45. *Without change.*
6. "The Nobility of Failure": Appeared with rather major cuts under the title "Le Japon de la mort choisie" in *L'Express*, March 1, 1980; reprinted here in its complete form and under its original title. *Without change.*
7. "Fur-bearing Animals": Written in 1976, these pages were intended for a collection of feminist texts to have been entitled *Les Coléreuses. Unpublished.*
8. "Mirror-Games and Will-o'-the-Wisps": *Nouvelle Revue française* 269 (May 1975), 1–15. *Without change.*
9. "On Some Erotic and Mystic Themes of the *Gita-Govinda*": *Cahiers du Sud* 342 (Sept. 1957), 218–28. Written as the preface

to a new translation of the *Gita-Govinda*, illustrated with re-
productions of medieval Hindu sculpture (Paris: Emile Paul,
1957). Reissued as an offprint by Rivages/Cahiers du Sud
(Marseilles, 1982). *Changed somewhat.*

10. "Festivals of the Passing Year"
    "Commentary on Christmas": *Le Figaro*, Dec. 22, 1976, 30.
    Without change.
    "The Days of Easter: One of the World's Most Beautiful
    Stories": *Le Figaro*, April 7, 1977, 1. *Without change.*
    "Fires of the Solstice": Originally titled "Fêtes oubliées," *Le
    Figaro*, June 22, 1977, 30. *Without change.* (A small addition
    has been made by the author for this English translation.)
    "Days of the Dead": Written in 1982. *Unpublished.*

11. "Who Knows Whether the Spirit of Animals Goes Down-
    ward": Appeared in Portuguese translation in *Raiz e Utopia*
    17–19 (Lisbon, 1981). The text is a lecture given by Yourcenar
    at the Gulbenkian Foundation, Lisbon, April 8, 1981. *Un-
    published in French.*

12. "The Sinister Ease of Dying": *Le Figaro*, Feb. 10, 1970, 1.
    Without change.

13. "Andalusia, or the Hesperides": Originally titled "Regard
    sur les Hespérides," *Cahiers du Sud* 315 (1952). Reissued as
    an offprint by Rivages/Cahiers du Sud (Marseilles, 1982).
    Changed somewhat.

14. "Oppian, or the Chase": Written as the preface to the *Cy-
    négétique d'Oppien* in the translation of Florent Chrestien and
    with original engravings by Pierre-Yves Trémois (Paris: Les
    Cent-Une, 1955), pp. I–VI. *Changed somewhat.*

15. "A Civilization in Watertight Compartments": *Le Figaro*, Feb.
    16, 1972, 1. *Without change.*

16. "Approaches to Tantrism": Originally titled "Des recettes
    pour un art du mieux vivre," *Le Monde*, July 24, 1972, 13.
    Some changes and additions.

17. "Written in a Garden": Originally published in a limited
    edition by Fata Morgana (Montpellier, 1980). *Changed some-
    what.*

18. "Tributes"

"In Memory of Diotima: Jeanne de Vietinghoff": *Revue mondiale*, Feb. 15, 1929, 413–18. *Without change.*

"Sketch for a Portrait of Jean Schlumberger": *Nouvelle Revue française* (March 1, 1969), 321–26. *Without change.*

"Tribute to Jacques Masui": Written in 1976. *Unpublished.*